SIR WALTER RALEIGH

SELECTIONS

From his Writings and Letters

Oxford University Press

*London Edinburgh Glasgow New York
Toronto Melbourne Cape Town Bombay*
Humphrey Milford *M.A. Publisher to the University*

From the painting in the NATIONAL PORTRAIT GALLERY

SIR WALTER RALEIGH

SIR WALTER RALEIGH

SELECTIONS

From his *Historie of
the World*, his
LETTERS
etc.

EDITED

With Introduction and Notes
By *G. E. Hadow*

OXFORD
AT THE CLARENDON PRESS
1 9 1 7

16320

EDITOR'S PREFACE

THE text of Letter II (pp. 177–81) is printed from the only known MS. in All Souls' College Library by the kind permission of the Librarian, Professor Oman.

To Mr. Percy Simpson I am indebted for the most careful revision of the text of the Selections throughout. He has contributed the section dealing with this in the Introduction and also the critical notes on the text, the facsimile letter, and the map. In fact, my debt to him is not for assistance but for collaboration, and I gladly take this opportunity to express my warm gratitude for all that this little book owes to his scholarship.

Cordial thanks are also due to Mr. Frederick Page, who checked the text of letters which are printed from MSS. in the British Museum and the Public Record Office.

CONTENTS

INTRODUCTION

TO most of us the Elizabethan Age stands for one of two things : it is the age of jewelled magnificence, of pomp and profusion and colour, of stately ceremonial and court pageant, of poetry and drama ; or it is the age of enterprise and exploration, of privateers and gentlemen adventurers, the age when Drake

> singed his Catholic Majesty's beard,
> And harried his ships to wrack,

when Gilbert and Cavendish and Frobisher sailed unknown seas, when Raleigh 'thought it to belong unto the honour of our Prince and Nation that a few Islanders should not think any advantage great enough against a fleet set forth by Q. Elizabeth '. Raleigh, perhaps more than any other, unites the two conceptions ; Raleigh with his hatband of pearls, his white satin pinked vest and jewelled shoes, one of the greatest courtiers, the greatest admirals, the greatest soldiers, and the greatest explorers of his day, who also found time to be an active member of Parliament, a poet, a musician, and an historian, and spent his leisure time at sea in the study of chemistry to such effect that he discovered ' the Great Elixer ' and was called upon to prescribe for the heir to the throne when the court physicians had given up all hope. It would be difficult for one man to touch life at more points. And in addition he exercised a fascination over his contemporaries, the glamour of which has not yet wholly faded. He had bitter enemies, and at least one false friend ; his position as court favourite naturally drew upon him much envy, and he was too true an Elizabethan not to be more deeply concerned in political intrigues than seems compatible, according to our present standards, with the manliness and nobility of character which he exhibited at other times. 'All rising to great place is by a winding stair,' wrote Bacon (who had reason to know), and Raleigh's path was by no means always straight. And yet with all this he was, and is, one of the most attractive figures in history. His popularity among his own men was such that in 1592, when ' the great Carrack ' taken from Portugal arrived at Dartmouth and it was found impossible to keep the populace from looting her, Raleigh had to be fetched from prison (where he was suffering temporary disgrace, having offended the queen by his marriage) as the only person who could keep order. 'I assure you, Sir,' writes Robert Cecil, ' his poor servants, to the number of a hundred and forty goodly men, and all the mariners, came to him with such shouts and joy as I never saw a man more troubled to quiet them in my life.' Two hundred years after Raleigh's first voyage to Guiana the Indians still looked for his return, as our ancestors looked for that of King Arthur. In dealing with the natives he had sternly insisted that his men should pay for everything they took, and that they should behave towards the inhabitants, and especially towards the women, with courtesy. The contrast between this treatment and that meted out to them by the Spaniards made them regard Raleigh as a sort of demi-god. One old chieftain, Topiawari, of his own wish 'gave me', writes Raleigh, 'his only son to take with me to England; and hoped that though he himself had but a short time to live, yet that by our means his son should be established after his death'. Such relations between an explorer and the aborigines go far to explain the success of English colonization.

The place which he filled in contemporary imagination is shown by the readiness with which the chief credit of any work with which he was associated was invariably assigned to him. In the words of one of his biographers : ' The nature of the man was that he could touch nothing but immediately it appropriated itself to him. He is fabled to have been the first to import mahogany into England from Guiana. He set orange trees in the garden of his wife's uncle, Sir Francis Carew, at Beddington ; and he has been credited with their first introduction. The Spaniards first brought potatoes into Europe. Hariot and Lane first discovered them in North Carolina. He grew them at Youghal, and they became his. Hariot discoursed learnedly on the virtues of tobacco, and Drake conveyed the leaf to England. Ralegh smoked, and none but he has the repute of the fashion. He gave the taste vogue, teaching courtiers to smoke their pipes with silver bowls. . . . For words, ways, and doings, he was the observed of all observers.' [1]

[1] *Sir Walter Ralegh*, by W. Stebbing, chap. V, p. 49 (Clarendon Press, 1899).

The bare facts of his life are interesting enough. He was born in 1554 (1552 according to some of his biographers), and was the half-brother of two other famous sea-kings of Devon, Humphrey and Adrian Gilbert. His father was a stanch Protestant, and there is a tradition of his getting into serious trouble, which might well have cost him his life, by insisting on stopping an old woman as she was going to Mass and trying to convert her then and there in the road. Fluttered and angry she went on her way, and bursting into church, declared that a plot was on foot to 'burn their houses over their heads . . . except they would leave their beads, and give over holy bread and holy water'. Whereupon the congregation flung out of church, 'like a sort of wasps,' and gave chase to Walter Raleigh the elder, who was rescued with difficulty by the mariners of Exeter.[1] Possibly it was from his father that Raleigh imbibed some of his hatred of his Catholic Majesty and the Spanish Inquisition. Nothing is known of his boyhood. He was for a time at Oriel College, Oxford, but he must have left the university very young, for in 1569 (when he cannot possibly have been more than seventeen) he was campaigning in France under one of the Champernouns (a kinsman of his mother). According to one tradition he was in Paris at the time of the massacre of St. Bartholomew (August 24, 1572), and in company with Philip Sidney took refuge in the house of Walsingham, the English Ambassador. There is no evidence to confirm this story, but at all

[1] For a full account of this incident see the *Life of Ralegh* by E. Edwards, vol. i, chap. I, pp. 16, 17 (Macmillan & Co., 1868).

events it is certain that for some years he fought in the Huguenot wars against the Catholics. He was back in England in 1577, and a little over a year later had his first experience of naval warfare, being given a command under his half-brother, Sir Humphrey Gilbert. The expedition was a failure, and the queen forbade its reorganization. The Spanish Government was already beginning to lodge formal complaints against Raleigh.

First sea-fight, 1579.

In 1580 he went to Ireland. His detestation of Catholicism, combined with a fierce hatred of rebels, possibly accounts for his share in the merciless suppression of the Irish. He took part in the brutal massacre of the Spanish and Italian garrison at Smerwick, and must bear some responsibility for the inhuman methods by which England sought to keep order. No wonder that he wrote later with considerable asperity : ' Her Majesty hath good cause to remember that a million hath bynn spent in Irland not many yeares since. A better kingdome might have bynn purchased att a less prize.' [1] Yet even in Ireland Raleigh knew how to win the affection and loyalty of his men. There is a delightful and characteristic story of his twice risking his life in a medley to save a fellow Devonian, one Henry Moyle, who had the bad luck twice to founder in the bog : ' At one moment he was unhorsed, and stood, with his pistol and quarter-staff, one man against twenty. But he extricated all his band without further loss than that of his horse.' [2]

Ireland, 1580.

In 1581 he was sent back to London with dispatches,

At Court, 1582.

[1] *Life of Ralegh*, Edwards, vol. ii, Letters xxxv, p. 79.
[2] Ibid., vol. i, chap III, p. 39.

and it was at this time that he first attracted the attention of Elizabeth. The well-known story of his spreading his new plush cloak upon ' a plashy place ' that the queen might pass over dryshod is of uncertain origin, but, true or not, it is eminently characteristic of both the chief actors. An act of picturesque gallantry would always come natural to Raleigh, and he would have a very shrewd perception of its probable effect upon Elizabeth. In any case, whether by this means or, as another tradition says, by the eloquence and wit with which he spoke before the queen in council, he did gain her favour and his rise was rapid. He acted as Elizabeth's confidential secretary, he was employed in more than one delicate negotiation, he became Warden of the Stanneries (which gave him authority over the rich tin mines of Cornwall), Vice-Admiral of Devon and Cornwall, Captain of the Yeomen of the Guard, Lord Chancellor (of all amazing offices), and to these honourable, but not all highly lucrative dignities, he added various minor posts, the profits of which enabled him to indulge in silver armour set with diamonds, rubies, and pearls, and shoes said to be worth ' more than six thousand six hundred gold pieces '. His taste for magnificence stood him in good stead with his royal mistress, who loved profusion so long as she had not to pay for it. All Raleigh's money, however, was not spent on fine clothes. Already he was busy with plans for planting English colonies in America, and only the queen's express command kept him from personally taking part in the fatal voyage of 1583, when Sir Humphrey Gilbert took formal possession of Newfoundland, but was lost, with his ship, on the way home. Raleigh spent considerable sums in encouraging such ventures, being granted in 1584 a charter empowering him, 'his heirs and assigns . . . to discover such remote heathen and barbarous lands, not actually possessed by any Christian prince, nor inhabited by Christian people, as to him or them shall seem good, to hold the same with all prerogatives, commodities, jurisdictions, royalties, and privileges by sea and land as We by letters patent may grant'. The same charter further permitted him and his heirs, not only ' to enjoy for ever the soil of such lands ', but ' to repel by land or sea all persons that shall without his or their liking attempt to inhabit the said Countries . . . giving also power to him or them to take those persons, with their ships and goods, and keep them as lawful prize, who without his or their licence shall be found trafficking within the limits aforesaid '. When the claim of Spain to dominion over the New World is considered, it is small wonder that Raleigh, with this charter in his pocket, found himself in constant antagonism with the Spaniards. In April 1584 he equipped two ships and sent them on a voyage of discovery to America. They explored the fertile land to which Elizabeth herself gave the name of Virginia, and the following year Raleigh sent out a larger fleet, under his cousin, Sir Richard Grenville, to plant a colony there. By a series of mischances the colony eventually proved a failure, but this was no fault of Raleigh's.

Late in 1591 or early in 1592 he incurred the queen's displeasure by a clandestine marriage with Elizabeth

Colonies, 1584.

Marriage, 1591–2.

Throgmorton, one of her maids of honour. Elizabeth was always furious that any of her favourites should dare to fall in love with any one but herself, and Raleigh was confined to the Tower. He eventually ransomed himself by means of the treasure of 'the great Carrack', to which reference has already been made. While still in disgrace, though no longer a prisoner, he busied himself with fresh **Voyage to** schemes of colonization, and in February 1595 he set out **Guiana,** on the famous voyage to Guiana of which he himself **1595.** has left a graphic account. It was this expedition which inspired him with faith in the mineral wealth of America, with visions of El Dorado, of mountains of gold and crystal; visions which later were to find such tragic issue.

He came back filled not only with plans for planting colonies and extending English dominions beyond the seas, but with a conviction that Spain meditated the speedy invasion of England, and he was not slow in endeavouring to stir up his countrymen to forestall the Spaniards. A naval expedition was equipped, but was delayed by **Cadiz,** contrary winds, and it was not until June 1596 that it **1596,** finally set sail for Cadiz. Raleigh was absent when the Council of War decided on the plan of attack, and when he came back from his task of rounding up stray Spanish ships he found Essex in the act of embarking soldiers on a rough sea with a view to attacking the town. One boat had already been swamped. Raleigh dissuaded him from this act of folly, and drew up and sent to Lord Thomas Howard, the High Admiral, a scheme of operations which was accepted. The action which ensued brought him some glory and some envy, but little else : 'What the Generals have gotten, I know least ; they protest it is little. For my own part I have gotten a lame leg and a deformed.' The naval victory was so complete that when the English troops landed after it they easily took possession of the town. Raleigh, wounded as he was, insisted on being carried ashore on his men's shoulders. A great part of the town was destroyed and its fortifications were dismantled, and then the expedition sailed home.

Raleigh's immediate reward was restoration to the queen's favour : 'Elizabeth used him very graciously, and gave him full authority to execute his place as Captain of the Guard. This he immediately undertook, and swore many men into void places.' [1] In addition to this court-soldiering he was actively engaged in strengthening the coast defences and preparing for further conflict with Spain. A second expedition was fitted out and placed The under the command of Essex, Lord Thomas Howard, Island and Raleigh. After vexatious delays, due to contrary voyage, winds, the fleet got away on August 17, 1597 and sailed 1597. for the Canaries. Rough weather drove the ships apart, and Raleigh, who expected to have joined forces with Essex at Fayal, found himself there alone. He waited for three days, and then attacked the enemy single-handed. His description of the battle will be found among the extracts from the *History of the World*. Essex found it difficult to forgive Raleigh for attacking without him, thus gaining all the credit of the victory, and, thanks in no small part to the activity of mischief-makers, a bitter

---

[1] *Sir Walter Ralegh*, Stebbing, chap. XIII, p. 133.

feud sprang up between the two. The brilliant rivals necessarily clashed at every turn, and the jealous and impatient disposition of Essex made him specially quick to suspect affronts. It is the more tragic that when he fell (four years later), Raleigh, as Captain of the Guard, **Execution of Essex, 1601.** had to be on duty at his execution. Through delicacy he withdrew into a distant room, and it is said that he afterwards regretted having done so, as he was told that Essex wished to be reconciled to him on the scaffold.

The two years that followed the death of Essex at once carried Raleigh to the summit of his prosperity and paved the way for his fall. He stood higher than ever in the queen's favour, he was busied with a host of public and private affairs, and amidst all his schemes for further explorations, his care for home defences, and the active share he took in legislation, he found time to be a patron of letters and—if report speaks true—to institute those famous nights at the Mermaid Tavern when the wits of the age met together to bandy jests, and a chance guest might see

> the singer of the *Faërie Queene*
> Quietly spreading out his latest cantos
> For Shakespeare's eye, like white sheets in the sun.
> Marlowe, our morning star, and Michael Drayton
> Talked in that ingle-nook. And Ben was there
> Humming a song upon that old black settle.

It was no wonder that many men envied Raleigh, and that there were some who plotted his ruin. The queen was old and was unmarried, and the question of the succession was becoming more and more urgent. The choice lay between James, son of Mary Queen of Scots (representing the Protestant party), and Arabella Stuart, the daughter of Darnley's younger brother (representing the Catholics). There were endless intrigues and counter-intrigues, but it became evident that the balance of probability lay in the direction of James, and those courtiers who wished to secure their position found themselves in a delicate situation. The mere suggestion that a successor would ever be required roused Elizabeth to fury; at the same time the new king, when he should enter upon his inheritance, was likely to look with favour upon those who had supported his claims while matters were yet unsettled. The result of all this was secret correspondence between more than one member of the English court and the King of Scotland. Already there was jealousy between those who were intriguing with James, each being anxious to secure the foremost place for himself. Among the men in whom the king most confided were Robert Cecil, who had long been a trusted and intimate friend of Raleigh ('I shall fly to you in all my cumbars as to the shurest staf I trust to in Sur Wattar's absens,' Lady Raleigh wrote to him in 1595), and Lord Henry Howard, Raleigh's bitter enemy, a spy in the pay of Philip who was not even faithful in his treachery, but corresponded with Spain and Scotland simultaneously. Cecil seems to have decided that Raleigh would prove a dangerous rival, and, while still professing friendship, deliberately set himself to instil distrust in the king's mind. This was rendered easier by

the fact of the old antagonism between Raleigh and Essex
—Essex having been an acknowledged supporter of James.
Raleigh himself had corresponded with Scotland, but
when, in 1601, the Duke of Lennox came on a mission to
England and approached certain of the leading courtiers,
terms were offered to Raleigh which he boasted of refusing.
The details of the story are obscure, but there is no doubt
that Cecil and Howard succeeded in poisoning the king's
mind against Raleigh and Cobham : ' I do profess,'
Cecil writes, ' in the presence of Him that knoweth and
searcheth all men's harts, that if I dyd not sometyme cast
a stone into the mouth of these gaping crabbs when they
are in their prodigall humour of discourses they wold
not stick to confess dayly how contrary it is to their
nature to resolve to be under your soverainty,' and this
though Cobham was his own brother-in-law and Raleigh
was a friend of years' standing with whom he was at the
moment corresponding about partnership in privateering
ventures.

Death of
Elizabeth,
1603.   Elizabeth died on March 24, 1603. Raleigh, who was
wholly ignorant of Cecil's correspondence concerning
him, signed a letter of welcome to James and rode
northwards, with many others, to meet him.   James
received him coldly, and very soon he was made to
realize that he was out of favour.   Various monopolies
which he had been granted were recalled, and his post
of Captain of the Guard was given to Sir Thomas
Erskine.   It was not long before he became involved in
far more serious trouble.

Spain stood before the world as the champion of

Catholicism, and Spanish gold was said to be employed
on behalf of Arabella Stuart. Philip's daughter, Isabella,
and the Archduke Albert were joint sovereigns of the
Low Countries, and had as minister a certain Count of
Arenberg, with whom Cobham had an old acquaintance.
Cobham undoubtedly carried on negotiations of some
sort with him, and Raleigh was said to be involved.
That Raleigh should appear as a supporter of Spain and
Catholicism was, to say the least, surprising, but his
enemies professed to believe in his complicity and he was
committed to the Tower. Cobham first turned king's
evidence to save his own skin, and then—too late—
repented of his ' barbarousness in accusing him falsely '.
There is no space here in which to enter into details
of the trial. That Raleigh knew something of Cobham's
intrigues is certain ; that he in any way instigated or
shared them was never proved. Coke, the Attorney-
General, who appeared for the crown, treated him
throughout with the utmost insolence and brutality :
' Thou hast a Spanish heart, and thyself art a spider of
hell,' is a fair sample of his invective, and it was obvious
from the first that the judgement was a foregone conclusion. ' The justice of England ', says Mr. Justice Gawdy,
' has never been so injured and degraded as by the
condemnation of Sir Walter Raleigh.' He defended
himself with spirit and dignity. ' Never man ', writes
Toby Matthew, ' spoke better for himself. So worthily,
so wisely, so temperately he behaved himself that in
half a day the mind of all the company was changed from
the extremest hate to the extremest pity.' But wisdom

and temperateness were of no avail to save the man whom the king feared. Raleigh was found guilty of high treason, and condemned to death with all the hideous detail of the time. The execution was fixed for December 13, and on December 9 Raleigh wrote to bid farewell to his wife the touching letter which is reprinted in this selection.

Imprison-
ment,
1603–16.

At the last moment, however, James changed his mind, and Raleigh was reprieved and sent to the Tower. Henry IV of France wrote to his ambassador in England to ask if the reprieve were due to Spanish gold, and if Cecil were concerned in it. Possibly Cecil did exert his influence to save from death the man he had betrayed. Certainly it was owing to his good offices that Raleigh was not reduced to beggary, and that his wife and child were provided for. His imprisonment had certain alleviations. Lady Raleigh, whose devotion to her husband never wavered, was allowed to be with him, and after a time he was moved from the damp, unhealthy apartments in which he was first confined to the Bloody Tower, where he had access to the governor's garden and was allowed (to Waad's annoyance) to turn the hen-house into a chemical laboratory. Here he spent twelve years in constant activity, reading, writing, experimenting, and making frequent efforts to obtain his freedom. His most powerful advocate was Prince Henry, who was his constant friend and often consulted him on important matters of state. The death of this prince, in November 1612, was a severe blow to his hopes.

There is something magnificent about a man who, ruined, disgraced, and imprisoned, can calmly sit down to write a *History of the World*. The very title gives a measure of the boundless ambition, the ignoring of all limitations, which mark the true Elizabethan. It is true that Raleigh himself realized that it was impossible actually to write the history of the whole world, but his plan, which embraced the history of the successive civilizations of the world, was sufficiently vast. He was continuing his keen interest in politics, he was planning fresh ventures in Guiana when he should be free, he was experimenting in chemistry, and in the midst of it all he sets out to write a gigantic work which displays a truly amazing amount of learning and research and is full of shrewd observations on men and life. That he was indebted to many friends for help and advice Raleigh frankly confesses. Dr. Robert Burhill (a noted rabbinical scholar), ' the acute and ingenious Sir John Hoskyns,' Hariot, the mathematician, and Ben Jonson himself are among those who are said to have assisted him. In his Preface Raleigh answers the objections of those who may complain against his use of Hebrew, ' in which language others may think, and I myself acknowledge it, that I am altogether ignorant : but it is true that some of them I find in *Montanus*, others in Latin character in *S. Senensis*, and of the rest I have borrowed the interpretation of some of my friends.' But when all allowance is made for the liberal borrowings in which authors of that day saw no reason to take shame, the book remains characteristically Raleigh's own, a monument not only of learning

History of the World.

and industry but of good sense and manly feeling, adorned with all the charm and dignity of seventeenth-century prose at its best. It must have helped Raleigh to pass many weary hours in the Tower, but in spite of its merits, it was scarcely a book to raise its author in the good graces of King James. James considered that kings held their authority direct from the Almighty, and any criticism directed against them by a subject was not only disloyal but impious—the fact that the sovereign in question had been dead for some centuries made no difference. The quaint words of the *Minde of the Front* (said to be from the pen of Ben Jonson) were not likely to conciliate him :—

> High Providence would so : that nor the Good
> Might be defrauded, nor the Great secur'd,
> But both might know their wayes are understood,
> And the reward, and punishment assur'd.

The punishment of the great was not, in the king's opinion, at all a suitable matter for discussion.[1]

Raleigh intended to trace the rise and fall of the great empires of the world. Book I begins with the creation of man and treats of the history of the Israelites in their earlier stages, and of the origin of Egyptian and Grecian mythology, and ' the beginning and establishing of Government '. Book II opens with the birth of Abraham,

---

[1] As a matter of fact James attempted to suppress the book. On Dec. 22, 1614, the Archbishop of Canterbury wrote to the Stationers' Company stating that he had ' express direction from his Majesty that the book latlie published by Sr Walter Rawleigh, nowe prisoner in the Tower, should be suppressed and not suffered for hereafter to be sould '.

discusses the various Egyptian dynasties and the oppression of the Israelites in Egypt, discourses learnedly on the meaning and value of law, and brings the Children of Israel into the Promised Land, where it leaves them while it goes back to treat of Deucalion and Phaeton. The middle of the book is concerned with the history of Troy, and later it goes on to summarize the wars of the Kings of Israel and Judah, breaks off to describe the founding of Rome, and finally ends with the destruction of Jerusalem by the Chaldeans. Book III deals with Babylon and with the wars of the Medes and Persians, passing on to the history of Greece and her wars against Darius and Xerxes, and devoting considerable space to Alexander. It ends with the death of Pyrrhus. Book V deals with the gradual establishment of the Roman empire.

He intended to add two more volumes, but these were never completed.[1]

Great as this work was, it did not—as has already been pointed out—absorb all the energies of its author. Raleigh never ceased to cherish dreams of a golden empire beyond the seas, and more than once he tried to persuade Queen Anne—always disposed to be his friend—to use her influence with the king that he might again attempt a voyage to Guiana. James, not unnaturally, desired both gold and empire, and gradually he came to believe that the enterprise at best might bring him wealth and power

[1] Two obviously apocryphal, and mutually contradictory, legends exist which state that Raleigh did complete his work but destroyed the last two volumes.

and at worst might rid him of a troublesome enemy whom public feeling would not permit him to execute off-hand. Cecil was dead, and Sir Ralph Winwood, the Secretary of State, was friendly to Raleigh. Lord Henry Howard, bitterest of all Raleigh's foes, died in June 1614, and George Villiers, the king's favourite, was inclined to befriend him out of sheer opposition to the Howards, whom he hated. Finally, in March 1616, a warrant was issued to 'permit Sir Walter Raleigh to go abroad to make preparations for his voyage'.

Last
Voyage,
1617.

He set sail on June 12, 1617, with thirteen ships and a thousand men under his command, knowing that his life depended upon a successful issue. From the first things went badly. Sickness fell upon the little company in Raleigh's ship. The weather was 'unnatural', so that 'the way that hath ever been sailed in fourteen days' was 'now hardly performed in fourtie days'.[1] Worst of all, he knew that political intrigues were at work all round him. The French Ambassador, realizing how the injustice with which Raleigh had been treated must rankle, had done his best to attach him to French interests in the hope that, should he find gold mines in Guiana, he might bethink him that there were other sovereigns less ungrateful than James. The Spaniards, while professing to see no harm in a peaceful voyage in search of a gold mine, were not forgetful of Raleigh's earlier career. They offered a safe conduct for two unarmed ships. Raleigh knew better than to walk into so obvious a trap,

[1] *Life of Ralegh*, Edwards, vol. ii, Letters cliii, p. 348. Sir Walter to Lady Raleigh.

but by his refusal of the offer he gave colour to the statement that he was in reality bent on a privateering expedition. James kept peace with Spain by sacrificing Raleigh. Before the little fleet set sail the Spanish Ambassador was furnished with a copy of the Survey made of it for the king. No wonder Raleigh writes with bitterness of ' the diligent care at London to make our strength known to the Spanish king ' that he might be able ' to fortifie all enterances against us '.

One bright spot only was there in that unhappy voyage : Raleigh's elder and dearly loved son, Wat, sailed with his father as captain of the flag-ship. With them also sailed Captain Keymis, a devoted follower who had been with Raleigh on the earlier voyage, and who professed to know the situation of the famous gold mine. They reached Lancerota (one of the Grand Canaries) on September 6. The inhabitants, mistaking them for Barbary pirates, who were just then terrorizing the islands, received them with hostility, and refused to allow them to water. It was here that young Wat first distinguished himself. Going ashore with half a dozen stout fellows, he put forty of the islanders to flight and succeeded in obtaining the much-needed water. In the light of later events there is something intensely pathetic in the eagerness with which Raleigh writes to the boy's mother : ' Your son had never so good health, having no distemper in all the heat under the Line.' The narrative of the rest of the voyage is given in Raleigh's letter to Sir Ralph Winwood. One ship deserted him at Lancerota, and its Captain, Baily, went home to hide his own shame by spreading false reports of his Admiral : several others were damaged by storms and had to delay for repairs. Sickness lay heavy upon them, and Raleigh himself was so ill of fever that his comrades despaired of his life. What was left of the fleet reached the mouth of the Orinoco in November. Here Raleigh—still severely shaken by illness—remained to guard the entrance to the river, while a landing party under his nephew, George Raleigh, and young Walter pushed on to find the mine, Keymis being their guide. Since the earlier expedition great changes had taken place in the Spanish settlement. Unknown to Raleigh the old city of San Thome had been deserted, and a new San Thome had sprung up directly in the path to the mine. Conflict with the Spaniards was inevitable. The English fell into an ambuscade, and among those killed was young Walter, who fell as he was gallantly leading his men. ' . . . my son,' writes Raleigh, ' (having more desire of honor than of safety) was slayne, with whome, to say the truth, all respect of the world hath taken end in me.' San Thome was taken, but the English appear to have become nervous and disorganized. Not till a week after the occupation did Keymis set out for the mine itself, though he declared it was only eight miles distant. Once more a successful ambuscade was prepared, and Keymis turned back, as he said, for more men. Evidently the responsibility was too much for him. George Raleigh held out for some time longer and pushed farther up the river, but although he won some spoil he did not find the mine.

When Keymis returned and announced his failure,

Raleigh realized that not only his life but his reputation was forfeit. He told Keymis that he must answer to the king and state, and upbraided him bitterly. Keymis, whose worst fault seems to have been that he was no leader, and whose devotion to Raleigh was beyond all question, passed a day or two in miserable excuses and explanations, and then, in despair, shot himself. Raleigh, too proud to seek so easy an escape, sailed home to face certain death and disgrace. He had promised, so he said later, whether he made a good voyage or a bad, to return to England.

No sooner had the news of the fight at San Thome reached England than the Spanish Ambassador presented himself before James with an accusation of piracy. And James at once accepted it as proven. Ignoring the fact that the Spaniards struck the first blow, the King of England described the attempt of his subjects to defend their lives as ' an horrible invasion of the town of S. Thome ' and ' a malicious breaking of the Peace '. There is no need to dwell upon the sequel. On his return to England, Raleigh was arrested by Sir Lewis Stukeley—Sir Judas Stukeley as he became known to his contemporaries. After a miserable period of spying and treachery, he was attainted of high treason, and on October 29, 1618, he was executed. As he walked to the scaffold, holding his white head erect in spite of the ague which had shaken him for two days past, he noticed in the crowd a venerable-looking man standing with bald head uncovered. Raleigh plucked the cap from his own thick, curly locks and flung it towards him, crying : ' You need this, my friend, more

Execution, 1618.

than I do.' It is said that when, according to custom, his head was shown to the people, a perceptible shudder ran through the crowd, and a voice cried out : ' We have not such another head to be cut off.'

There has been no space in which to enlarge upon one of the most beautiful and touching sides of Raleigh's life—his relations with his wife—but it is impossible to close without reference to the brave and loyal-hearted woman who shared her husband's imprisonment, and who never wearied of fighting his battles. The letters that passed between them are full of tenderness. This brief sketch may well end with one written by Lady Raleigh to her brother, Sir Nicholas Carew, just after her husband's execution :

' I desiar, good brother, that you will be plessed to let me berri the worthi boddi of my nobell hosban, Sur Walter Ralegh, in your chorche at Beddington, wher I desiar to be berred. The Lordes have geven me his ded boddi, though they denied me his life. This ni(gh)t hee shall be brought you with two or three of my men. Let me here presently. God hold me in my wites '.[1]

E. R.'

[1] *Life of Ralegh,* Edwards, vol. ii, p. 413.

THE TEXT

The selections made in this edition are reprinted from contemporary texts and manuscripts, all of which are authoritative. No autograph text of any of the letters has been found, but they are reprinted either from official copies in the Public Record Office or from careful transcripts made for two eminent collectors, Sir Robert Cotton, the antiquary, and Archbishop Sancroft. The following is a detailed statement of the sources of the texts.

The History of the World

The extracts from the *History* are taken from the first edition, published in folio in 1614. It was entered on the Stationers' Register on April 15, 1611, but the printer, William Stansby, and the publisher, Walter Burre, evidently had difficulty in producing the book. It was issued anonymously with an engraved and emblematic title-page, containing the short title, *The History of the World. At London. Printed for Walter Burre*, 1614. A second edition followed in the same year.

The Last Fight of the Revenge

The text follows the original edition issued anonymously in quarto in 1591 ; the title-page is reproduced in facsimile before the reprint. This edition was entered on the Stationers' Register on November 23, 1591, and was evidently written in that month, as the reference on page 158, l. 4 shows. The running title is *The last fight of the Revenge at sea.* Richard Hakluyt reprinted the work in 1599. In 1598 he began to issue the second edition of his great collection of English voyages of discovery and adventure. Next year there appeared *The Second Volume of the Principal Nauigations, Voyages, Traffiques and Discoueries of the English Nation, made by Sea or ouer land, to the South and South-east parts of the World, at any time within the compasse of these* 1600. *yeres.* Raleigh's tract appears on pages 169–76 (numbered over twice in the erratic paging of this edition) with this title : *A report of the trueth of the fight about the Isles of Açores, the last of August 1591. betwixt the Reuenge, one of her Maiesties shippes, and an Armada of the king of Spaine ; Penned by the honourable Sir Water Ralegh knight.* This is our authority for ascribing the tract to Raleigh. It is interesting to note that Hakluyt edited the tract, making slight but careful corrections : he alters inaccurate figures, misspelt Spanish names, and once or twice a lapse in Raleigh's grammar.[1]

The Letters

I. *The Action in Cadiz Harbour.* This was first printed by Raleigh's grandson, Philip, in 1699, from a draft found among Sir Walter's papers. But the present reprint follows the interesting transcript in Tanner MS. 278 of the Bodleian (folios 240–4) made for Archbishop Sancroft, and by him minutely collated with the autograph ; it is slightly more correct than the printed text. Sancroft added to the title ' Transcrib'd from a MS. in the Hands of his Grandchild, Mr Raleigh', and worked carefully over the text, revising even the details of spelling and punctuation. Two corrections are interesting : in the famous passage which describes how the Earl of Essex threw his hat into the sea, Philip Raleigh made his grandfather shout out *Entramus ;* Sancroft corrects the Latin to Spanish—*Entramos* (p. 168, l. 24) ; and near the end, where the Spanish ships were said to be ' committed into ashes ' (p. 176, l. 29), Sancroft corrects ' converted into ashes '. There are a number of minor variants.

[1] See the notes, pp. 201 ff.

II. Raleigh's letter to his wife when he attempted suicide in the Tower, on July 18, 1603, is taken from MS. 155 (folios 100 verso–102) in the Library of All Souls College, Oxford. Major Martin Hume, in his monograph on *Sir Walter Raleigh*, p. 262, has expressed some doubt about the authenticity of this 'pathetic and beautiful letter', as he rightly calls it. The transcript is in a seventeenth-century hand; there is nothing, either in the contents or the style, which makes the ascription to Raleigh transparently impossible; and in view of the fact that the attempt at suicide has been discredited as a slander set afloat by Raleigh's enemies, it may be noted that Major Martin Hume holds there can be 'no reasonable doubt' that the attempt was made. Those who dispute the authenticity of the transcript probably regard it as an invention based on the letter which immediately follows in this selection.

III. Raleigh's letter to his wife in December 1603, when he expected to be executed, is taken from Sloane MS. 3520 (folios 14–17) in the British Museum. This manuscript is a collection of letters by Raleigh transcribed for Sir Robert Cotton. Other transcripts are to be found in Harleian MS. 4761 (folios 20 verso–22), which is evidently a first draft, and in the *Domestic State Papers of James I*, 1603, vol. xcvi, no. 71, preserved in the Public Record Office, and among the *Cecil Papers* at Hatfield. The text of the Sloane MS. is fuller and is evidently genuine. The official copy in the *State Papers* shows signs of editing; there are two significant omissions:

(1) 'To what freind to direct thee, I knowe not, for all mine have left mee, in the true tyme of triall; And I plainely perceive, that my death was determyned from the first day' (p. 182, ll. 17–20.).

The official copy was probably taken before the letter left the Tower: did Raleigh contrive to add later this severe reflection on Cecil's scheming and the king's justice? The Cecil copy has this sentence, but the Harleian copy has not.

(2) In the following passage the parts enclosed in square brackets are omitted : '[Gett those Letters (if it bee possible) which I writt to the Lords, wherein] I sued for my life, God is my wittnesse, Itt was for you and yours I desired life. [Butt itt is true that I disdaine my selfe for begging itt]' (pp. 183–4).

The letters to which he refers may be read in Edwards's *Life*; there is in these appeals something craven and ignoble, which contrasts with the splendid courage he showed at all other times and in the hour of death. It is easy to see why he wished to suppress them ; but how did he evade the official transcriber, especially in such a nice point as half a sentence ? Further, he had here the skill to baffle Cecil, whose copy does not contain the bracketed words. Nor are they in the Harleian copy.

Two minor corrections of the Cecil, Harleian, and Record Office copies may also be due to editing : (1) Instead of ' death, and all his mishapen and ouglye shapes ' (p. 184, ll. 4, 5) they read ' ouglie formes ', which is no doubt what Raleigh intended to write; (2) Instead of ' The everlasting, powerfull, infinite and omnipotent god, that Almightie God ' (ib. ll. 14–15), they also correct the repetition by reading ' infinite and inscrutable god '. The other variants are insignificant.

IV. Raleigh's letter to Sir Ralph Winwood, in March 1618, reporting the failure of the Guiana voyage, is taken from the official transcript in the *Domestic State Papers of James I*, 1618, vol. xcvi, no. 70. The first two leaves of this manuscript have been torn in the margin ; the missing words, enclosed in square brackets, are supplied from another official transcript in the *Cecil Papers*, the readings of which are generally supported by transcripts in Sloane MS. 3520 (folios 5–10) and Harleian MS. 4761 (folios 13–18). One sentence (p. 189, ll. 27–8) is defective in both copies : the words 'left them' are a stopgap inserted by Edwards. The Cecil transcript has a number of variants, but perhaps only one is important : in the passage explaining the failure to work the mine (p. 189, ll. 2–5) the text here followed reads 'although I know not (his Majestie excepted) whome I am to satisfie so much as my self, having lost my sonne, and my estate in the enterprise ', the Cecil transcript substitutes for the opening words ' although I know his Majesty expects '— a far from lucid variant. The Harleian transcript approximates to the Cecil, but reads ' expect ': the Sloane MS. gives the sentence a new turn, thus—' I knowe his Majestie (whom I am to satisfy) expects not at my hands soe muche, my self haveing lost ', &c.

V. Raleigh wrote to his wife the day after writing the preceding letter. The best text is in Sloane MS. 3520 (folios 2–4) of the British Museum, from which Letter III has been reprinted. There is a transcript in another British Museum MS., Harleian 4761 (folios 23–5), which differs chiefly in omitting words. When Raleigh sat down to write, he intended to send his wife only a brief letter of consolation; but he opened the letter again, and added in a postscript a succinct account of the failure, which she was to communicate to others as his authoritative statement.

VI. The letter to the king written on September 24, 1618, is taken from the official copy in the *Domestic State Papers of James I*, 1618, vol. xcix, no. 69 1. There is another copy in the same volume (no. 70), with some interesting variants.

In two points the text has been normalized : *j* and *v* are printed in accordance with the usage of the present day, and contractions such as ' y^e ' and ' coṁand ' have been expanded. Such misprints as ' beeeing ', ' shinning ' (for ' shining ') have been tacitly corrected.

This autograph letter, preserved among the *Domestic State Papers* of Queen Elizabeth's reign, was written on July 26, 1597. A facsimile is given to show Raleigh's handwriting. The text is as follows:

Sr I hvmbl[i]e thanke yow for your letters, I can add
nothinge of substance to the generall letter, I only
se[n]d thes to reme[m]ber my love & service,
my L : Generall is my guest in the wast spight, the
Earle of Ruttland, Sr Thomas Germayne Alexander Rattc-
life, & Sr R Mansfelde, I should have taken it vnkynd-
ly if my lorde had taken vp a[n]y other lodging till
the lion cum, & now her Maiestye may be sure
his L : shall sleape somewhat the sovnder though
hee farr the wors by being wth me, for I am
an excelent watchman att sea
wee only atte[n]d the winde havinge repayred as mich
as wee can our bruses, butt wee shall not be in any
great Corage for winter weather & longe nights
in thes shipps.
I trust wee shall pforme what soever & more can
be dvn wth like strenght & means, Sr I pray love
vs in your element & wee will love & honor yow in
ours & every wher. & remayne to be cõmanded by you
for evermore
W Ralegh.

Sr I pray vouchsaef to re[mem]ber me
in all affection to my lorde
Cobham

plymouth the 26.
of July

Raleigh follows the contemporary practice of using marks of abbreviation: the omission of *n* or *m* was commonly indicated by placing a stroke over the preceding vowel (as in 'cõmanded'), and in writing 'send', 'remember', 'any', 'attend', Raleigh perhaps meant the stroke with which he continues the *a* or *e* to denote this abbreviation. His spelling was not faultless.

The occasion of the letter was as follows. Philip of Spain was known to be preparing a reprisal for the brilliant attack made on Cadiz in 1596. It was decided to anticipate his attack by a second expedition which started on July 10, 1597. Essex—'my Lord General' of the letter—was in command. But the expedition was dispersed by a gale and driven back. Raleigh's letter was written at this stage.

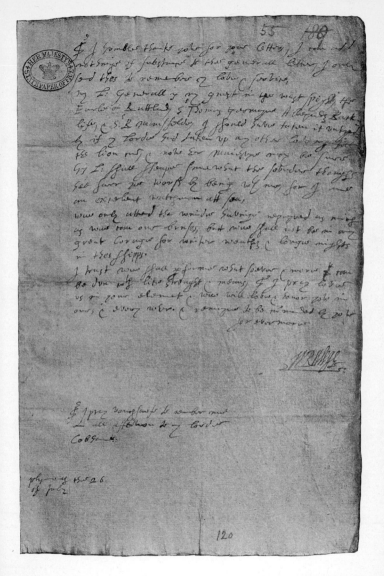

55   480

120

Letter of RALEIGH to CECIL

THE

HISTORIE OF

THE WORLD.

§ I.

The Preface.

HOw unfit, and how unworthy a choice I have made
of my self, to undertake a worke of this mixture;
mine owne reason, though exceeding weake, hath sufficiently resolved me. For had it beene begotten then
with my first dawne of day, when the light of common
knowledge began to open it selfe to my yonger yeares:
and before any wound received, either from Fortune or
Time: I might yet well have doubted, that the darkenesse
of Age and Death would have covered over both It and
Mee, long before the performance. For, beginning with
the Creation: I have proceeded with the History of the
World; and lastly purposed (some few sallies excepted)
to confine my Discourse, with this our renowned Iland
of *Great Brittaine*. I confesse that it had better sorted
with my dissability, the better part of whose times are
run out in other travailes; to have set together (as I could)

the unjoynted and scattered frame of our English affaires,
than of the universall: in whome had there beene no other
defect, (who am all defect) then the time of the day, it
were enough; the day of a tempestuous life, drawne on
to the very evening ere I began. But those inmost, and
soule-peircing wounds, which are ever aking while uncured:
with the desire to satisfie those few friends, which I have
tried by the fire of adversitie; the former enforcing, the
latter perswading; have caused mee to make my thoughts
legible, and my selfe the Subject of every opinion wise 10
or weake.

To the world I present them, to which I am nothing
indebted: neither have others that were, (Fortune
changing) sped much better in any age. For, Prosperity
and Adversity have ever-more tied and untied vulgar
affections. And as we see it in experience, That dogs doe
alwaies barke at those they know not; and that it is in
their nature to accompany one another in those clamours:
so it is with the inconsiderate multitude. Who, wanting
that vertue which we call Honesty in all men, and that 20
especiall gift of GOD which we call Charity in Christian
men; condemne, without hearing; and wound, without
offence given: led there-unto by uncertaine report only;
which his *Majesty* truely acknowledgeth for the Author
of all lies.* *Blame no man* (saith Siracides †) *before thou have
inquired the matter: understand first, and then reforme
righteously.* Rumor, res sine teste, sine iudice, maligna,
fallax; *Rumor is without witnesse, without judge, malicious
and deceiveable.* This vanity of vulgar opinion it was, that

* *Dæmonolog. l. 3. c. 1.*   † *Eccl. c. 11. v. 7.*

gave Saint *Augustine* Argument to affirme, That he feared
the praise of good men, and detested that of the evill.*
And heerein no man hath given a better rule, then this
of *Seneca ; Conscientiæ satisfaciamus : nihil in famam
laboremus ; sequatur vel mala, dum benè mereraris. Let us
satisfie our owne consciences, and not trouble our selves with
fame : be it never so ill, it is to be despised so we deserve well.*†

For my selfe, if I have in any thing served my Country,
and prised it before my private : the generall acceptation
10 can yeeld me no other profit at this time, than doth
a faire sunshine day to a Sea-man after shipwrack ; and
the contrary no other harme than an outragious tempest
after the port attained. I know that I lost the love of
many, for my fidelity towardes Her, whom I must still
honor in the dust ; though further than the defence of
Her excellent person, I never persequuted any man. Of
those that did it, and by what device they did it : He that
is the Supreame Judge of all the world, hath taken the
accompt ; so as for this kind of suffering, I must say
20 with *Seneca, Mala opinio, benè parta, delectat.*

As for other men ; if there be any that have made
themselves Fathers of that fame, which hath beene begotten
for them : I can neither envy at such their purchased
glory, nor much lament mine owne mishap in that kind ;
but content my selfe to say with *Virgil, Sic vos non vobis,*
in many particulars.

To labour other satisfaction, were an effect of phrenzie,
not of hope : seeing it is not Truth, but Opinion, that

* *Laudari à bonis timeo, & amari à malis detestor.*
† *Sen. de ira. l. 3. c. 22.*

can travaile the world without a passeport. For were it otherwise ; and were there not as many internall formes of the minde, as there are externall figures of men ; there were then some possibility, to perswade by the mouth of one Advocate, even Equity alone.

But such is the multiplying and extensive vertue of dead Earth, and of that breath-giving life which GOD hath cast upon Slime and Dust : as that among those that were, of whom we reade and heare, and among those that are, whom we see and converse with ; every one hath received a severall picture of face, and everie one a diverse picture of minde ; every one a forme apart, every one a fancy and cogitation differing : there being nothing wherein Nature so much triumpheth, as in dissimilitude. From whence it commeth, that there is found so great diversity of opinions ; so strong a contrariety of inclinations ; so many naturall and unnaturall ; wise, foolish ; manly, and childish affections, and passions in Mortall Men. For it is not the visible fashion and shape of plants, and of reasonable Creatures, that makes the difference, of working in the one, and of condition in the other ; but the forme internall.

And though it hath pleased GOD, to reserve the Art of reading mens thoughts to himselfe : yet, as the fruit tels the name of the Tree ; so doe the outward workes of men (so farre as their cogitations are acted) give us wherof to guesse at the rest. Nay, it were not hard to expresse the one by the other, very neare the life : did not craft in many, feare in the most, and the worlds love in all, teach every capacity, according to the compasse it hath, to qualifie and maske over their inward deformities for a time. Though it be also true, *Nemo potest diu personam ferre fictam : cito in naturam suam recidunt, quibus veritas non subest. No man can long continue masked in a counterfeit behaviour : the thinges that are forced for pretences, having no ground of truth, cannot long dissemble their owne natures.* Neither can any man (saith *Plutarch*) so change himselfe, but that his heart may be sometime seene at his tongues end.

10   In this great discord and dissimilitude of reasonable creatures, if wee direct our selves to the Multitude ; *Omnis honestæ rei malus iudex est vulgus, The common people are evill Judges of honest things,* and *whose wisdome* (saith Ecclesiastes) *is to bee despised*; if to the better sort ; every understanding hath a peculiar judgment, by which it both censureth other men, and valueth it selfe. And therefore unto mee it will not seeme strange, though I finde these my worthlesse papers torne with Rats : seeing the slouthfull Censurers of all ages, have not spared 20 to taxe the Reverend Fathers of the Church, with Ambition ; the severest men to themselves, with Hypocrisie ; the greatest lovers of Justice, with Popularity ; and those of the truest valour and fortitude, with vaineglorie. But of these natures, which lie in wayt to finde fault, and to turne good into evill, seeing *Salomon* * complained long since : and that the very age of the world renders it every day after other more malitious ; I must leave the professors to their easie waies of reprehension, than which there is nothing of more facility.†

* Eccl. c. 11.   † *Nihil facilius, quam reprehendere alium.*

To me it belongs in the first part of this præface,
following the common and approved custome of those
who have left the memories of time past to after ages;
to give, as neare as I can, the same right to History which
they have done. Yet seeing therein I should but borrow
other mens wordes; I will not trouble the Reader with
the repetition. True it is, that among many other
benefits, for which it hath beene honored; in this one
it triumpheth over all humane knowledge, That it hath
given us life in our understanding, since the world it 10
selfe had life and beginning, even to this day: yea it
hath triumphed over time, which besides it, nothing but
eternity hath triumphed over: for it hath carried our
knowledge over the vast and devouring space of many
thousands of yeares, and given so faire and peircing
eies to our minde; that we plainely behould living now,
as if we had lived then, that great World, *Magni Dei
sapiens opus, the wise worke* (saith Hermes) *of a great
GOD*, as it was then, when but new to it selfe. By it
I say it is, that we live in the very time when it was 20
created: we behold how it was governed: how it was
covered with waters, and againe repeopled: How Kings
and Kingdomes have florished and fallen; and for what
vertue and piety GOD made prosperous; and for what
vice and deformity he made wretched, both the one and
the other. And it is not the least debt which we owe
unto History, that it hath made us acquainted with our
dead Ancestors; and, out of the depth and darkenesse
of the earth, delivered us their memory and fame. In
a word, wee may gather out of History a policy no lesse 30

wise than eternall ; by the comparison and application
of other mens fore-passed miseries, with our owne like
errours and ill deservings.

But it is neither of Examples the most lively instructions, nor the words of the wisest men, nor the terror
of future torments, that hath yet so wrought in our blind
and stupified mindes ; as to make us remember, That the
infinite eye and wisdome of GOD doth peirce through all
our pretences ; as to make us remember, That the justice
10 of GOD doth require none other accuser, than our owne
consciences : which neither the false beauty of our apparent actions, nor all the formallitie, which (to pacifie the
opinions of men) we put on ; can in any, or the least
kind, cover from his knowledge. And so much did that
Heathen wisdome confesse, no way as yet qualified by
the knowledge of a true GOD. If any (saith Eurypides)
having in his life committed wickednesse, thinke hee can
hide it from the everlasting gods, he thinkes not well.

To repeat GODS judgements in particular, upon those
20 of all degrees, which have plaied with his mercies ; would
require a volume apart : for the *Sea* of examples hath no
bottome. The markes, set on private men, are with their
bodies cast into the earth ; and their fortunes, written
onely in the memories of those that lived with them :
so as they who succeed, and have not seene the fall of
others, doe not feare their owne faults. GODS judg-
ments upon the greater and greatest, have beene left to
posterity ; first, by those happy hands which the Holy
Ghost hath guided ; and secondly, by their vertue, who
30 have gathered the acts and ends of men, mighty and

remarkeable in the world. Now to poynt farre off, and
to speake of the conversion of Angells into Deuills, for
Ambition : Or of the greatest and most glorious Kings,
who have gnawne the grasse of the earth with beasts, for
pride and ingratitude towards GOD : Or of that wise
working of *Pharao*, when he slue the Infants of *Israel*,
ere they had recovered their Cradles : Or of the policy
of *Jezabel*, in covering the murder of *Naboth* by a triall
of the *Elders*, according to the Law : with many thousands
of the like : what were it other, than to make an hopelesse 10
proofe, that farre-off examples would not be left to the
same farre-off respects, as heretofore ? For who hath not
observed, what labour, practise, perill, bloudshed, and
cruelty, the Kings and Princes of the world have under-
gone, exercised, taken on them, and committed ; to make
them-selves and their issues maisters of the world ? And
yet hath *Babylon*, *Persia*, *Egypt*, *Syria*, *Macedon*, *Carthage*,
Rome, and the rest, no fruit, no flower, grasse, nor leafe,
springing upon the face of the Earth, of those seedes :
No ; their very roots and ruines doe hardly remaine. 20
Omnia quæ manu hominum facta sunt, vel manu hominum
evertuntur, vel stando & durando deficiunt : All that the
hand of man can make, is either overturnd by the hand of
man, or at length by standing and continuing consumed.
The reasons of whose ruines, are diversly given by those
that ground their opinions on second causes. All Kingdomes and States have fallen (say the Politicians) by
outward and forraine force, or by inward negligence and
dissension, or by a third cause arising from both : Others
observe, That the greatest have suncke downe under their 30

owne weight; of which *Livie* hath a touch: *eo crevit, ut magnitudine laboret sua* : Others, That the divine providence (which *Cratippus* objected to *Pompey*) hath set downe the date and period of every estate, before their first foundation and erection. But hereof I will give my selfe a day over to resolve.

For seeing the first bookes of the following story, have undertaken the discourse of the first Kings and King-domes : and that it is impossible for the short life of a Preface, to travaile after and over-take farr-off Antiquity, and to judge of it ; I will, for the present, examine what profit hath been gathered by our owne Kings, and their Neighbour Princes : who having beheld, both in divine and humane letters, the successe of infidelitie, injustice, and crueltie ; have (notwithstanding) planted after the same patterne.

True it is that the judgements of all men are not agreeable ; nor (which is more strange) the affection of any one man stirred upp a-like with examples of like nature : But every one is touched most, with that which most neerely seemeth to touch his owne private ; Or otherwise best suteth with his apprehension. But the judgements of GOD are for ever unchangeable ; neither is he wearied by the long processe of time, and won to give his blessing in one age, to that which he hath cursed in another. Wherefore those that are wise, or whose wise-dome, if it be not great, yet is true and well grounded ; will bee able to discerne the bitter fruites of irreligious policie, as well among those examples that are found in ages removed farre from the present, as in those of latter

times. And that it may no lesse appeare by evident
proofe, than by asseveration, That ill doing hath alwaies
beene attended with ill successe ; I will here, by way of
preface, runne over some examples, which the worke
ensuing hath not reached. . . .

Oh by what plots, by what forswearings, betrayings,
oppressions, imprisonments, tortures, poysonings, and
under what reasons of State, and politique subteltie, have
these forenamed Kings, both strangers, and of our owne
Nation, pulled the vengeance of GOD upon them-selves, 10
upon theirs, and upon their prudent ministers ! and in the
end have brought those things to passe for their enemies,
and seene an effect so directly contrarie to all their owne
counsailes and cruelties ; as the one could never have
hoped for themselves ; and the other never have succeeded ; if no such opposition had ever beene made. GOD
hath said it and performed it ever : *Perdam sapientiam
sapientum, I will destroy the wisdome of the wise.*

But what of all this ? and to what end doe we lay before
the eies of the living, the fal and fortunes of the dead : 20
seeing the world is the same that it hath bin ; and the
children of the present time, wil stil obey their parents ?
It is in the present time, that all the wits of the world
are exercised. To hold the times we have, we hold all
things lawfull : and either we hope to hold them for ever ;
or at least we hope, that there is nothing after them to
bee hoped for. For as wee are content to forget our owne
experience, and to counterfeit the ignorance of our owne
knowledge, in all things that concerne our selves ; or
perswade our selves, that GOD hath given us letters 30

patents to pursue all our irreligious affections, with a *non obstante* : so wee neither looke behind us what hath beene, nor before us what shall bee. It is true, that the quantitie which wee have, is of the body : wee are by it joyned to the earth : we are compounded of earth ; and wee inhabite it. The Heavens are high, farr off, and unsearcheable : wee have sense and feeling of corporal things ; and of eternall grace, but by revelation. No mervaile then that our thoughts are also earthlie : and 10 it is lesse to be wondred at, that the words of worthlesse men cannot cleanse them : seeing their doctrine and instruction, whose understanding the Holy Ghost vouchsafed to inhabite, have not performed it. For as the Prophet *Esai* cryed out long agone, *Lord, who hath beleeved our reports* ? And out of doubt, as *Esai* complained then for him selfe and others : so are they lesse beleeved, every day after other. For although Religion, and the truth thereof, bee in every mans mouth, yea in the discourse of every woman, who for the greatest 20 number are but *Idolls of vanitie* : what is it other than an universall dissimulation ? * Wee professe that wee know GOD : but by workes we deny him. For Beatitude doth not consist in the knowledge of divine things, but in a divine life : for the Devills know them better than men. *Beatitudo non est divinorum cognitio, sed vita divina.* And certainly there is nothing more to bee admired, and more to bee lamented, than the privat contention, the passionate dispute, the personall hatred, and the perpetuall warre, massacres, and murders, for

* *Paule to Titus Ch. i. ve. 10.*

Religion among *Christians* : the discourse whereof hath
so occupied the World, as it hath well neare driven the
practise thereof out of the world. Who would not soone
resolve, that tooke knowledge but of the religious disputa-
tions among men, and not of their lives which dispute,
that there were no other thing in their desires, than the
purchase of Heaven ; and that the World it selfe were but
used as it ought, and as an Inne or place, wherein to
repose our selves in passing on towards our celestiall
habitation ? when on the contrary, besides the discourse 10
and outward profession, the soule hath nothing but
hypocrisie. Wee are all (in effect) become Comædians
in religion : and while we act in gesture and voice,
divine vertues, in all the course of our lives wee renounce
our Persons, and the parts wee play. For Charitie,
Justice, and Truth, have but their being *in termes*, like
the Philosophers *Materia prima*.

Neither is it that wisedome, which *Salomon* defineth
to be the *Schoole-Mistresse of the knowledge of God*, that
hath valuation in the world : it is enough that we give 20
it our good word ; but the same which is altogether
exercised in the service of the World, as the gathering
of riches cheifly ; by which we purchase and obtaine
honour, with the many respects which attend it.

These indeed bee the markes, which (when wee have bent
our consciences to the highest) wee all shoote at. For the
obtayning whereof it is true, that the care is our owne ;
the care our owne in this life, the perill our owne in the
future : and yet when we have gathered the greatest
aboundance, wee our selves enjoy no more thereof, than 30

so much as belongs to one man. For the rest; Hee that had the greatest wisedome, and the greatest ability that ever man had, hath told us that this is the use : *When goods increase* (saith Salomon *) *they also increase that eate them ; and what good commeth to the Owners, but the beholding thereof with their eyes ?* As for those that devour the rest, and follow us in faire weather : they againe forsake us in the first tempest of misfortune, and steere away before the Sea and Winde ; leaving us to the malice of our
10 destinies. Of these, among a thousand examples, I will take but one out of Maister *Dannet*, and use his owne words : *Whilest the Emperour* Charles *the fift, after the resignation of his Estates, stayed at* Vlushing *for winde, to carrie him his last journie into Spaine ; Hee conferred on a time with* Seldius, *his brother* Ferdinands *Embassadour, till the deepe of the night. And when* Seldius *should depart : the Emperour calling for some of his servants, and no bodie answering him (for those that attended upon him, were some gone to their lodgings, and all the rest a sleepe) the Emperour*
20 *tooke up the candle him-selfe, and went before* Seldius *to light him downe the staires ; and so did, notwithstanding all the resistance that* Seldius *could make. And when Hee was come to the staires foot, He said thus unto him :* Seldius, *remember this of* Charles *the Emperour, when hee shalbe dead and gone, That Him, whome thou hast knowne in thy time environed with so many mighty Armies, and Guards of souldiors, thou hast also seene alone, abandoned, and for-saken, yea even of his owne domesticall servants. &c.* I acknowledge this change of Fortune to proceed from the

* Eccless. 5. 11.

*mighty hand of GOD; which I will by no meanes goe about
to withstand.*

But you will say that there are some things else, and of
greater regard than the former. The first, is the reverend
respect that is held of great men, and the Honour done
unto them by all sorts of people. And it is true indeed :
provided, that an inward love for their justice and piety,
accompany the outward worship given to their places
and power ; without which what is the applause of the
Multitude, but as the outcrie of an Heard of *Animals*, 10
who without the knowledge of any true cause, please
them-selves with the noyse they make ? For seeing it is
a thing exceeding rare, to distinguish Vertue and Fortune :
the most impious (if prosperous) have ever beene ap-
plauded ; the most vertuous (if unprosperous) have ever
beene despised. For as Fortunes man rides the Horse,
so Fortune her-selfe rides the *Man.* Who, when hee is
descended and on foote : the Man taken from his Beast,
and Fortune from the Man ; a base groome beates the
one, and a bitter contempt spurnes at the other, with 20
equall libertie.

The second, is the greatning of our posterity, and the
contemplation of their glory whom wee leave behinde us.
Certainly, of those which conceive that their soules
departed take any comfort therein, it may be truly said
of them, which *Lactantius* spake of certaine Heathen
Philosophers, *quod sapientes sunt in re stulta.** For when
our spirits immortall shalbe once separate from our
mortall bodies, and disposed by GOD : there remaineth

* *Lact* : *de falsa sap.* 3. *c.* 29.

in them no other joy of their posterity which succeed, than there doth of pride in that stone, which sleepeth in the Wall of a Kings Palace ; nor any other sorrow for their povertie, than there doth of shame in that, which beareth up a Beggars cottage. . . . And whatsoever comfort shall remaine of all forepast, the same will consist in the charitie, which we exercised living : and in that Pietie, Justice, and firme Faith, for which it pleased the infinite mercy of GOD to accept of us, and receive us. Shall we
10 therefore value honour and riches at nothing ? and neglect them, as unnecessarie and vaine ? certainlie no. For that infinite wisdome of GOD, which hath distinguished his Angells by degrees : which hath given greater and lesse light, and beautie, to Heavenly bodies : which hath made differences betweene beasts and birds : created the Eagle and the flie, the Cedar and the Shrub : and among stones, given the fairest tincture to the Rubie, and the quickest light to the Diamond ; hath also ordained Kings, Dukes or Leaders of the people, Magistrates,
20 Judges, and other degrees among men. And as honour is left to posteritie, for a marke and ensigne of the vertue and understanding of their Ancestors : so, seeing *Siracides* * preferreth Death before Beggerie : and that titles, without proportionable estates, fall under the miserable succour of other mens pittie ; I accompt it foolishnesse to condemne such a care : Provided, that worldly goods bee well gotten, and that wee raise not our owne buildings out of other mens ruines. For, as *Plato* † doth first preferre the perfection of bodilie health ; secondly, the forme and

* *Sira. c.* 40. *v.* 28.   † *Plat. de leg.* 1. 2. 6. & *in Gorgea.*

beautie; and thirdly, *Divitias nulla fraude quæsitas*: so Hieremie* cries, *Woe unto them that erect their houses by unrighteousnesse, and their chambers without equitie*: and Esai † the same, *Woe to those that spoyle and were not spoyled*. And it was out of the true wisdome of *Salomon*,‡ that hee commandeth us, *not to drinke the wine of violence; not to lie in wait for bloud; and not to swallow them up alive, whose riches wee covet: for such are the wayes* (saith hee) *of every one that is greedy of gaine*.

And if wee could afford our selves but so much leisure as to consider, That hee which hath most in the world, hath, in respect of the world, nothing in it: and that he which hath the longest time lent him to live in it, hath yet no proportion at all therein, setting it either by that which is past when wee were not, or by that time which is to come in which wee shall abide for ever: I say, if both, to wit our proportion in the world, and our time in the world, differ not much from that which is nothing; it is not out of any excellency of understanding, that wee so much prise the one, which hath (in effect) no being: and so much neglect the other, which hath no ending: coveting those mortall things of the world, as if our soules were therein immortall, and neglecting those things which are immortall, as if our selves after the world were but mortall.

But let every man value his owne wisdome, as hee pleaseth. Let the Rich man thinke all fooles, that cannot equall his aboundance; the Revenger esteeme all negli-

---

* Jer. 22. 13.   [† Esay 33.]
‡ Prov. 1. 18. 12.   Prov. 23. 1. 3. 8. 9. 25. 9. 8.

gent, that have not troden down their opposites; the Politician, all grosse, that cannot merchandize their faith: Yet when wee once come in sight of the Port of death, to which all winds drive us, and when by letting fall that fatall Anchor, which can never be weighed again, the Navigation of this life takes end: Then it is I say, that our owne cogitations (those sad and severe cogitations, formerly beaten from us by our Health and Felicitie) returne againe, and pay us to the uttermost for 10 all the pleasing passages of our lives past. It is then that wee crie out to GOD for mercie; then, when our selves can no longer exercise cruelty towards others: and it is onely then, that wee are strucken through the soule with this terrible sentence, *That GOD will not be mockt.** For if according to Saint *Peter*,† *The righteous scarcely bee saved: and that* GOD *spared not his Angells*: where shall those appeare, who, having served their appetites all their lives, presume to thinke, that the severe commandements of the All-powerfull GOD were given but in sport; and that the short 20 breath, which wee draw when death presseth us, if wee can but fashion it to the sound of *Mercy* (without any kinde of satisfaction or amends) is sufficient? *O quam multi*, saith a reverend Father, *Cum hac spe ad æternos labores & bella descendunt*: I confesse that it is a great comfort to our friends, to have it said, that wee ended wel; for wee all desire (as *Balaam* did) *to die the death of the righteous.* But what shall wee call a disesteeming, an apposing, or (indeed) a mocking of GOD; if those men doe not appose him, disesteeme him, and mocke him, that thinke it

* Gala. 6. 7. † Pet. 1. 4. [18.]

D 2

enough for God, to aske him forgivenesse at leisure, with the remainder and last drawing of a malitious breath? For what doe they other-wise, that die this kinde of well-dying, but say unto GOD as followeth? Wee beseech thee O GOD, that all the falshoods, forswearings, and treacheries of our lives past, may be pleasing unto thee; that thou wilt for our sakes (that have had no leisure to doe any thing for thine) change thy nature (though impossible) and forget to bee a just GOD; that thou wilt love injures and oppressions, call ambition wisdome, and charity foolishnesse. For I shall præjudice my sonne (which I am resolved not to doe) if I make restitution; and confesse my selfe to have been unjust, (which I am too proud to doe) if I deliver the oppressed. Certainly, these wise worldlings have either found out a new GOD; or made One: and in all likelihood such a Leaden One, as *Lewis* the eleventh ware in his Cappe; which, when he had caused any that he feared, or hated, to be killed, hee would take it from his head and kisse it: beseeching it to pardon him this one evill act more, and it should be the last; which (as at other times) hee did, when by the practice of a *Cardinall* and a falsified Sacrament, he caused the *Earle* of *Armagnack* to bee stabbed to death; mockeries indeed fit to be used towards a Leaden, but not towards the ever-living God. But of this composition are all the devout lovers of the world, that they feare all that is durelesse and ridiculous: they feare the plots and practices of their opposites, and their very whisperings: they feare the opinions of men which beat but upon shadowes: they flatter and forsake the prosperous and unprosperous, bee they friends or Kings : yea they dive under water, like Ducks, at every pebble stone, that's but throwne towards them by a powerfull hand : and on the contrary, they shew an obstinate and Giant-like valour, against the terrible judgements of the All-powerfull GOD : yea they shew themselves gods against GOD, and slaves towards men ; towards men whose bodies and consciences are alike rotten.

Now for the rest : If wee truly examine the difference of both conditions ; to wit of the rich and mighty, whome wee call fortunate ; and of the poore and oppressed, whome we account wretched : wee shall find the happinesse of the one, and the miserable estate of the other, so tied by GOD to the very instant, and both so subject to interchange (witnesse the suddaine downefall of the greatest Princes, and the speedy uprising of the meanest persons) as the one hath nothing so certaine, whereof to boast ; nor the other so uncertaine, whereof to bewaile it selfe. For there is no man so assured of his honour, of his riches, health, or life ; but that hee may be deprived of either or all, the very next houre or day to come. *Quid vesper vehat, incertum est, What the evening will bring with it, it is uncertaine. And yet yee cannot tell* (saith Saint James) * *what shalbe to morrow. To day he is set up, and to morrow hee shall not be found : for hee is turned into dust, and his purpose perisheth.* And although the aire which compasseth adversitie, be very obscure : yet therin wee better discerne GOD, than in that shining light which environeth worldly glorie ; through which, for the clearnesse thereof, there is no vanitie which escapeth our sight. And let

* Jam. 4. 14.

adversitie seeme what it will; to happie men, ridiculous,
who make them-selves merrie at other mens misfortunes;
and to those under the *crosse*, greivous: yet this is true,
That for all that is past, to the very instant, the portions
remaining are equall to either. For bee it that wee have
lived many yeares, *and* (according to *Salomon*) *in them
all wee have rejoyced*; or bee it that we have measured the
same length of daies, and therein have ever-more sorrowed:
yet looking backe from our present being, we find
both the one and the other, to wit, the joy and the woe, 10
sayled out of sight; and death, which doth pursue us
and hold us in chace, from our infancie, hath gathered it.
*Quicquid ætatis retro est, mors tenet: What-so-ever of our
age is past, death holds it.* So as who-so-ever hee bee, to
whome Fortune hath beene a servant, and the Time
a friend: let him but take the accompt of his memory
(for wee have no other keeper of our pleasures past) and
truelie examine what it hath reserved, either of beauty and
youth, or foregone delights; what it hath saved, that
it might last, of his dearest affections, or of what ever 20
else the amorous Spring-time gave his thoughts of con-
tentment, then unvaluable; and hee shall finde that all
the art which his elder yeares have, can draw no other
vapour out of these dissolutions, than heavie, secret, and
sad sighes. Hee shall finde nothing remaining, but those
sorrowes, which grow up after our fast-springing youth;
over-take it, when it is at a stand; and over-top it utterly,
when it beginnes to wither: in so much as looking
backe from the very instant time, and from our now being;
the poore, diseased, and captive creature, hath as little 30

sence of all his former miseries and paines; as hee, that
is most blest in common opinion, hath of his fore-passed
pleasures and delights. For what-so-ever is cast behind us,
is just nothing : and what is to come, deceiptfull hope
hath it : *Omnia quæ eventura sunt, in incerto iacent.*
Onely those few blacke Swannes I must except : who
having had the grace to value worldly vanities at no more
than their owne price; doe, by retayning the comfortable
memorie of a well acted life, behold death without dread,
10 and the grave without feare ; and embrace both, as
necessary guides to endlesse glorie.

For my selfe, this is my consolation, and all that I can
offer to others, that the sorrowes of this life, are but of
two sorts : whereof the one hath respect to GOD ; the
other, to the World. In the first wee complaine to GOD
against our selves, for our offences against him ; and confesse, *Et tu iustus es in omnibus quæ venerunt super nos,*
And thou O Lord art just in all that hath befallen us. In
the second wee complaine to our selves against GOD :
20 as if hee had done us wrong, either in not giving us
worldly goods and honours, answering our appetites :
or for taking them againe from us, having had them ;
forgetting that humble and just acknowledgment of
Job, The Lord hath given, and the Lord hath taken. To
the first of which Saint *Paul* hath promised blessednesse ;
to the second, death. And out of doubt hee is either
a foole or ungratefull to GOD, or both, that doth not
acknowledge, how meane so-ever his estate bee, that the
same is yet farre greater, than that which GOD oweth
30 him : or doth not acknowledge, how sharpe so-ever his

afflictions bee, that the same are yet farre lesse, than those which are due unto him. And if an Heathen wise man call the adversities of the world but *tributa vivendi, the tributes of living:* a wise Christian man ought to know them, and beare them, but as the tributes of offending. He ought to beare them man-like, and resolvedly; and not as those whining souldiors do, *qui gementes sequuntur imperatorem.*

For seeing God, who is the Author of all our tragedies, hath written out for us, and appointed us all the parts 10 we are to play: and hath not, in their distribution, beene partiall to the most mighty Princes of the world; That gave unto *Darius* the part of the greatest Emperour, and the part of the most miserable begger, a begger begging water of an Enemie, to quench the great drought of death; That appointed *Bajazet* to play the *Gran Signior* of the *Turkes* in the morning, and in the same day the *Footstoole* of *Tamerlane* (both which parts *Valerian* had also playd, beeing taken by *Sapores*) that made *Bellisarius* play the most victorious Captaine, and lastly 20 the part of a blinde beggar; of which examples many thousands may be produced: why should other men, who are but of the least wormes, complaine of wrongs? Certainly there is no other account to be made of this ridiculous world, than to resolve, That the change of fortune on the great Theater, is but as the change of garments on the lesse. For when on the one and the other, every man weares but his own skin; the Players are all alike. Now if any man, out of weaknes, prise the passages of this world otherwise (for saith *Petrarch, Magni ingenii* 30 *est revocare mentem a sensibus*) it is by reason of that unhappie fantasie of ours, which forgeth in the braines of Man all the miseries (the corporall excepted) whereunto hee is subject: Therein it is, that Misfortune and Adversitie worke all that they worke. For seeing Death, in the end of the Play, takes from all, whatsoever Fortune or Force takes from any one: it were a foolish madnes in the shipwracke of worldly things, where all sinkes but the Sorrow, to save it. That were, as *Seneca* saith, *Fortunæ* 10 *succumbere, quod tristius est omni fato, To fall under Fortune, of all other the most miserable destinie.*

But it is now time to sound a retrait; and to desire to be excused of this long pursuit: and withall, that the good intent, which hath moved me to draw the picture of time past (which we call *Historie*) in so large a Table, may also be accepted in place of a better reason. . . . . . .

I have beene already over long, to make any large discourse either of the parts of the following Story, or 20 in mine owne excuse: especially in the excuse of this or that passage; seeing the whole is exceeding weake and defective. Among the grosest, the unsutable division of the bookes, I could not know how to excuse, had I not been directed to inlarge the building after the foundation was laid, and the first part finished. All men know that there is no great Art in the deviding evenly of those things, which are subject to number and measure. For the rest, it sutes well enough with a great many Bookes of this Age, which speake to much, and yet say little; 30 *Ipsi nobis furto subducimur,* We are stollen away from our selves, setting a high price on all that is our owne. But hereof, though a late good Writer make complaint, yet shall it not lay hold on me, because I beleeve as he doth ; that who so thinkes himselfe the wisest man, is but a poore and miserable ignorant. Those that are the best men of war, against all the vanities and fooleries of the World, do alwaies keepe the strongest guards against themselves, to defend them from themselves, from selfe love, selfe estimation, and selfe opinion.

Generally concerning the order of the worke, I have onely taken counsaile from the Argument. For of the *Assyrians,* which after the downefall of *Babel* take up the first part, and were the first great Kings of the World, there came little to the view of posterity : some few enterprises, greater in fame than faith, of *Ninus* and *Semiramis* excepted.

It was the story of the *Hebrewes,* of all before the *Olympiads,* that overcame the consuming disease of time ; and preserved it selfe, from the very cradle and beginning to this day : and yet not so entire, but that the large discourses thereof (to which in many Scriptures wee are referred) are no where found. The Fragments of other Stories, with the actions of those Kings and Princes which shot up here and there in the same time, I am driven to relate by way of digression : of which we may say with *Virgil.*

Apparent rari nantes in gurgite vasto ;
They appeare here and there floting in the great gulfe of time.

To the same first Ages doe belong the report of many Inventions therein found, and from them derived to

us; though most of the Authors Names have perished
in so long a Navigation. For those Ages had their Lawes;
they had diversity of Government; they had Kingly
rule; Nobilitie, Pollicie in warre; Navigation; and all, or
the most of needfull Trades. To speake therefore of these
(seeing in a generall Historie we should have left a great
deale of Nakednesse, by their omission) it cannot properly
bee called a digression. True it is that I have also made
many others: which if they shall be layd to my charge,
10 I must cast the fault into the great heape of humane
error. For seeing wee digresse in all the wayes of our lives:
yea seeing the life of man is nothing else but digression;
I may the better bee excused, in writing their lives and
actions. I am not altogether ignorant in the Lawes of
Historie, and of the Kindes.

The same hath beene taught by many; but by no man
better, and with greater brevity, than by that excellent
learned Gentleman *Sir Francis Bacon.* Christian Lawes
are also taught us by the Prophets and Apostles; and
20 every day preacht unto us. But wee still make large
digressions: yea the teachers themselves do not (in all)
keepe the path which they poynt out to others.

For the rest; after such time as the *Persians* had
wrested the Empire from the *Chaldæans,* and had raised
a great Monarchie, producing Actions of more importance
than were else-where to be found: it was agreeable to
the Order of Story, to attend this Empire; whilest it so
florished, that the affaires of the nations adjoyning had
reference there-unto. The like observance was to bee used
30 towards the fortunes of *Greece,* when they againe began

to get ground upon the *Persians*, as also towards the affairs of *Rome*, when the *Romans* grew more mighty than the *Greeks*.

As for the *Medes*, the *Macedonians*, the *Sicilians*, the *Carthaginians*, and other *Nations* who resisted the beginnings of the former Empires, and afterwards became but parts of their composition and enlargement : it seemed best to remember what was knowne of them from their severall beginnings, in such times and places, as they in their flourishing estates opposed those Monar- 10 chies ; which in the end swallowed them up. And herein I have followed the best Geographers : who seldome give names to those small brookes, whereof many, joyned together, make great Rivers ; till such time as they become united, and runne in a maine streame to the Ocean *Sea*. If the Phrase be weake, and the Stile not every-where like it selfe : the first, shews their legitimation and true Parent ; the second, will excuse it selfe upon the Variety of Matter. For *Virgill*, who wrote his *Eclogues*, *gracili avena*, used stronger pipes when he sounded the 20 warres of *Æneas*. It may also bee layd to my charge that I use divers *Hebrew* words in my first booke, and else where : in which language others may thinke, and I my-selfe acknowledge it, that I am altogether ignorant : but it is true, that some of them I finde in *Montanus*, others in lattaine Carecter in S. *Senensis*, and of the rest I have borrowed the interpretation of some of my learned friends. But say I had beene beholding to neither, yet were it not to bee wondred at, having had a eleven yeares leasure, to attaine the knowledge of that, or of any other 30

tongue; How-so-ever, I know that it will bee said by many,
That I might have beene more pleasing to the Reader, if
I had written the Story of mine owne times; having
been permitted to draw water as neare the Well-head as
another.   To this I answer, that who-so-ever in writing
a moderne Historie, shall follow truth too neare the heeles,
it may happily strike out his teeth.   There is no Mistresse
or Guide, that hath led her followers and servants into
greater miseries.   He that goes after her too farre off,
10 looseth her sight, and looseth him-selfe : and hee that
walkes after her at a middle distance; I know not whether
I should call that kinde of course Temper or Basenesse.
It is true, that I never travailed after mens opinions,
when I might have made the best use of them : and I have
now too few daies remayning, to imitate those, that
either out of extreame ambition, or extreame cowardise,
or both, doe yet, (when death hath them on his shoulders)
flatter the world, betweene the bed and the grave.   It is
enough for me (being in that state I am) to write of the
20 eldest times : wherein also why may it not be said,
that in speaking of the past, I point at the present,
and taxe the vices of those that are yet lyving, in their
persons that are long since dead ; and have it laid to my
charge ?   But this I cannot helpe, though innocent.
And certainely if there be any, that finding themselves
spotted like the Tigers of old time, shal finde fault with
me for painting them over a new ; they shall therein
accuse themselves justly, and me falsly.

For I protest before the Majesty of GOD, That I malice
30 no man under the Sunne.   Impossible I know it is to

please all : seeing few or none are so pleased with them-selves, or so assured of themselves, by reason of their subjection to their private passions; but that they seeme diverse persons in one and the same day. *Seneca* hath said it, and so do I : *Unus mihi pro populo erat* : and to the same effect *Epicurus, Hoc ego non multis sed tibi*; or (as it hath since lamentably fallen out) I may borrow the resolution of an ancient Philosopher, *Satis est unus, Satis est nullus*. For it was for the service of that inestimable Prince *Henry*, the successive hope, and one of the greatest of the Christian World, that I undertooke this Worke. It pleased him to peruse some part thereof, and to pardon what was amisse. It is now left to the world without a Maister : from which all that is presented, hath received both blows and thanks. *Eadem probamus, eadem reprehendimus : hic exitus est omnis iudicii, in quo lis secundum plures datur.* But these discourses are idle. I know that as the charitable will judge charitably : so against those, *qui gloriantur in malitia,* my present adversitie hath disarmed mee. I am on the ground already; and therefore have not farre to fall : and for rysing againe, as in the Naturall privation there is no recession to habit ; so it is seldome seene in the privation politique. I doe therefore for-beare to stile my Readers *Gentle, Courteous,* and *Friendly,* thereby to beg their good opinions, or to promise a second and third volume (which I also intend) if the first receive grace and good acceptance. For that which is already done, may be thought enough ; and too much : and it is certaine, let us claw the Reader with never so many courteous phrases; yet shall we ever-more

be thought fooles, that write foolishly. For conclusion ;
all the hope I have lies in this, That I have already found
more ungentle and uncourteous Readers of my Love
towards them, and well-deserving of them, than ever
I shall doe againe. For had it beene otherwise, I should
hardly have had this leisure, to have made my selfe
a foole in print.

§ II.

[OF TRIUMPHAL ENTRIES.

10 *A discourse concerning Joas' triumphant entry into*
Jerusalem, with a brief account of the conduct
of Charles VIII in the City of Florence.]

WEe may justly marvaile how it came to passe, that
Joas, being thus in possession of *Jerusalem*, having
the King in his hands, his enemies forces broken, and his
own entire, could bee so contented to depart quietly, with
a little spoile, when hee might have seized upon the whole
Kingdome. The reigne of *Athalia* had given him cause
to hope, that the issue of *David* might be dispossessed of
20 that crowne ; his owne Nobilitie, being the sonne and
grand-childe of Kings, together with the famous actes that
hee had done, were enough to make the people of *Juda*
thinke highly of him ; who might also have preferred
his forme of government, before that of their owne
Kings, especially at such a time, when a long succession
of wicked Princes had smoothered the thankes, which
were due to the memorie of a few good ones. The commoditie that would have ensued, upon the union of all

the twelve Tribes, under one Prince, is so apparant, that
I need not to insist on it. That any message from God
forbad the *Israelites* (as afterwardes in the victorie which
Peka the son of *Romelia* got upon *Ahaz*) to turne his
present advantage, to the best use, wee doe not reade.
All this makes it the more difficult to resolve the question,
why a Prince so well exercised, as *Joas* had beene, in
recovering his owne, and winning from his enemie, should
forsake the possession of *Jerusalem*, and wilfully neglect
the possibilities, or rather cast away the full assurance 10
of so faire a conquest, as the Kingdome of *Juda*.

But concerning that point, which, of all others, had
beene most materiall, I meane the desire of the vanquished
people to accept the *Israelite* for their King, it is plainely
seene, that entring *Jerusalem* in triumphant manner, *Joas*
was unable to concoct his own prosperitie. For the
opening of the gates had beene enough to have let him
not only into the Citie, but into the royall throne,
and the peoples hearts, whom by faire intreatie (especially
having sure meanes of compulsion) hee might have 20
made his owne, when they saw themselves betrayed, and
basely given away by him whose they had beene before.
The faire marke which this opportunitie presented, he
did not aime at, because his ambition was otherwise and
more meanely busied, in levelling at the glory of a triumphant entrie through a breach. Yet this errour might
afterwards have been corrected well enough, if entring
as an enemie, and shewing what he could doe, by spending
his anger upon the walles, he had within the Citie done
offices of a friend, and laboured to shew good will to 30

the inhabitants. But when his pride had done, his covetousnesse began, and sought to please it selfe, with that which is commonly most readie to the spoiler, yet should be most forborne. The treasure wherewith *Sesac*, *Hazael*, and the *Philistims*, men ignorant of the true God and his religion, had quenched their greedie thirst, ought not to have tempted the appetite of *Joas*, who though an idolatour, yet acknowledged also and worshipped the eternall God, whose Temple was at 10 *Jerusalem*. Therfore when the people saw him take his way directly to that holy place, and lay his ravenous hands upon the consecrated vessels, calling the family of *Obed Edom* (*whose children had hæreditarie charge of the treasurie* *) to a strict account, as if they had beene Officers of his owne Exchequer, they considered him rather as an execrable Church-robber, than as a Noble Prince, an *Israelite* and their brother, though of another Tribe. Thus following that course, which the most vertuous King of our age (taxing it with the same phrase) 20 hath wisely avoyded; by stealing a few apples, hee lost the inheritance of the whole Orchard. The people detested him, and after the respite of a few dayes, might by comparing themselves one to one, perceive his Souldiers to be no better than men of their owne mould, and inferiour in number to the inhabitants of so great a Citie. It is not so easie to hold by force a mighty Town entered by capitulation, as to enter the gates opened by unadvised feare. For when the Citizens, not being disarmed, recover their spirits, and begin to understand their first

* 1 *Chron.* 26. 15.

errour ; they will thinke upon every advantage, of place, of provisions, of multitude, yea of women armed with tilestones, and rather chuse by desperate resolution, to correct the evils growne out of their former cowardice, than suffer those mischiefes to poyson the bodie, which in such halfe-conquests, are easily tasted in the mouth. A more lively example hereof cannot be desired, than the Citie of *Florence*, which through the weakenesse of *Peter de Medices*, governing therein as a Prince, was reduced into such hard termes, that it opened the gates unto 10 the French King *Charles* the eight, who not plainly professing himselfe either friend or foe to the Estate, entred the Towne, with his Armie, in triumphant manner, himselfe and his horse armed, with his lance upon his thigh. Manie insolencies were therin committed by the French, and much argument of quarrell ministred, betweene them and the Townes-men : so farre forth that the *Florentines*, to preserve their libertie, were driven to prepare for fight. To conclude the matter, *Charles* propounds intollerable conditions, demaunding huge 20 summes of readie monie, and the absolute Signorie of the State, as conquered by him, who entred the Citie in Armes. But *Peter Caponi*, a principall Citizen, catching these Articles from the Kings Secretarie, and tearing them before his face, bad him sound his trumpets, and they would ring their bels : which peremptorie wordes made the French bethinke themselves, and come readily to this agreement, that for fortie thousand pounds, and not halfe of that monie to be paid in hand, *Charles* should not onely depart in peace, but restore whatsoever 30

he had of their dominion, and continue their assured
friend. So dangerous a matter did it seeme for that
brave Armie, which in few moneths after wanne the
Kingdome of Naples, to fight in the streetes, against the
armed multitude of that populous Citie. It is true, that
Charles had other businesse (and so perhaps had *Joas*, as
shall anon be shewed) that called him away : but it was
the apprehension of imminent danger that made him
come to reason. In such cases, the firing of houses,
usually drawes everie Citizen to save his owne, leaving
victorie to the Souldier : yet where the people are prepared and resolved, women can quench, as fast as the
enemie having other things to looke unto, can set on
fire. And indeede that Commaunder is more given to
anger than regardfull of profit, who upon the uncertain
hope of destroying a Towne, forsakes the assurance of
a good composition. Diversitie of circumstance may
alter the case : it is enough to say, that it might be in
Jerusalem, as we know it was in *Florence*.

§ III.

[OF KEEPING FAITH.

*A discourse of that cunning perfidiousness and horrible
deceit of this latter age, called Equivocation.*]

OUt of the passage betweene *Josua* and the *Gibeonites*, the Doctrine of keeping Faith is so plainely
and excellently taught, as it taketh away all evasion,
it admitteth no distinction, nor leaveth open any hole

or out-let at all to that cunning perfidiousnesse, and
horrible deceit of this latter age, called *Æquivocation*.
For, notwithstanding that these *Gibeonites* were a people of
the *Hevites*,* expresly and by name, by the commandement
of God to be rooted out, and notwithstanding that they
were liers, and deceivers, and counterfeits, and that they
did over-reach, and as it were, deride *Josua*, and the
Princes of *Israel*, by faining to bee sent as Embassadours
from a farre Countrie, in which travaile their clothes
were worne; their bread mouldie, which they avowed to 10
have been warme for newnesse when they first set out;
their barrells and bottles of wine broken; their shoes
patcht; and their sacks rent and ragged † : Yet *Josua*
having sworne unto them by the Lord God of *Israel*,
hee durst not, though urged by the murmure of the
people, to lay violent hands on them; but hee spared
both their Lives, and the Cities of their inheritance.

Now if ever man had warrant to breake Faith, and to
retract his promise made, *Josua* had it. For first, the
commandement which hee received from God to roote 20
out this Nation among the rest, preceded by farre the
peace which hee had granted them. Secondly, he might
justly have put these men to the sword, and have sackt
their Cities; if there bee any evasion from a promise made,
whereof the living God is called to witnesse. For it was
not to the *Gibeonites* that hee gave peace, because hee
knew them to bee a people hated of God. Hee told them,
that if they were of the *Hevites*,‡ it was not in his power

---

* *Jos.* 9. 7.   † *Jos.* 9. from the 5. to the 13. *Vers*.
‡ *Jos.* 9. 7.

to make a league with them. But it was to a strange people that hee gave faith, and to a Nation which came from farre, who hearing of the wonders which the God of *Israel* had done in *Ægypt* and over *Jordan*, sought for peace and protection from his people. Thirdly, the accord, which *Israel* made with these craftie *Canaanites*, was without warrant.* For it is written in the same place, That the *Israelites* accepted their tale, that is, beleeved what they had said, *and counsailed not with the mouth of* 10 *the Lord*. Fourthly, these men who were knowne Idolaters, and served those Puppets of the Heathen, men of an Apish Religion, as all Worshippers of Images are, could not challenge the witnesse of the true God, in whome they beleeved not. I say therefore, that if ever man might have served himselfe by any evasion or distinction, *Josua* might justly have done it. For hee needed not in this case the helpe of *Æquivocation*, or *Mentall Reservation*. For what hee sware, hee sware in good Faith; but hee sware nothing, nor made any promise at all to the 20 *Gibeonites*. And yet, to the end that the faithlesse subtiltie of man should borrow nothing in the future from his example, who knowing well, that the promises hee made in the name of God, were made to the living God, and not to the dying Man, hee held them firme, and inviolable, notwithstanding that they, to whom hee had sworne it, were worshippers of the Devill.

For it is not, as faithlesse men take it, that he which sweareth to a Man, to a Societie, to a State, or to a King, and sweareth by the name of the living Lord, and in his

* *Jos.* c. 9. *vers.* 14.

presence, That this promise (if it bee broken) is broken to a Man, to a Societie, to a State, or to a Prince ; but the promise in the name of God made, is broken to God. It is God, that wee therein neglect: wee therein professe that wee feare him not, and that we set him at nought and defie him. If hee that without Reservation of honour giveth a lie in the presence of the King, or of his Superiour, doth in point of Honour give the lie to the King himselfe, or to his Superiour ; how much more doth he breake Faith with God, that giveth Faith in the presence of God, promiseth in his name, and makes him a witnesse of the Covenant made ?

Out of doubt, it is a fearefull thing for a Sonne to breake the Promise, Will, or Deed of the Father ; for a State, or Kingdome, to breake those Contracts which have beene made in former times, and confirmed by publique faith. For though it were 400. yeares after *Josua*, that *Saul*, even out of devotion, slaughtered some of those people descended of the *Gibeonites* : yet God who forgat not what the Predecessours and Fore-fathers of *Saul* and the *Israelites* had sworne in his name, afflicted the whole Nation with a consuming famine ; and could not be appeased, till seven of *Saules* sonnes were delivered to the *Gibeonites* grieved, and by them hanged up.

And certainely, if it be permitted by the helpe of a ridiculous distinction, or by a God-mocking equivocation, to sweare one thing by the name of the living God, and to reserve in silence a contrarie intent : the life of man, the estates of men, the faith of Subjects to Kings, of Servants to their Masters, of Vassalls to their Lords, of

Wives to their Husbands, and of Children to their
Parents, and of all trialls of right, will not onely be made
uncertaine, but all the chaines, whereby freemen are tied
in the world, be torne a sunder. It is by oath (when Kings
and Armies cannot passe) that we enter into the Cities
of our enemies, and into their Armies : it is by oath that
warres take ende, which weapons cannot ende. And what
is it or ought it to be that makes an oath thus powerfull,
but this ; That he that sweareth by the name of God,
10 doth assure others that his wordes are true, as the Lord of
all the World is true whom he calleth for a witnesse, and
in whose presence he that taketh the oath hath promised ?
I am not ignorant of their poore evasions, which play
with the severitie of Gods Commaundements in this kinde :
But this indeede is the best answere, That he breakes
no faith, that hath none to breake. For whosoever hath
faith and the feare of God dares not doe it.

The *Christians* in the *Holie Land* when they were at the
greatest, and had brought the *Caliph* of *Ægypt* to pay them
20 tribute, did not only loose it againe, but were soone after
beaten out of the *Holie Land* it selfe : by reason (saith
William of *Tyre*, a reverend Bishop which wrote that
storie) that *Almerick* the fift King after *Godfrey* brake
faith with the *Caliph Elhadech*, and his *Vicegerent*,
The *Soldan Sanar* ; who being sodainely invaded by
Almerick drew in the *Turke Syracon* to their aide :
whose Nephew *Seladine*, after he had made *Ægypt* his
owne, beate the *Christians* out of the *Holie Land* ; neither
would the wooden Crosse (the very *Crosse*, say they,
30 that *Christ* died on) give them victorie over *Seladine*,

when they brought it into the field as their last refuge:
seeing they had forsworne themselves in his name, that
was crucified thereon.   And if it bee a direction from the
holy Ghost, *That hee that speaketh lies, shall be destroied,* and
that *the mouth which uttereth them, slaieth the soule* : * how
much more perilous is it (if any perill be greater than to
destroy the soule) to sweare a lie ?   It was *Eugenius* the
Pope, that perswaded, or rather commanded the King of
Hungarie after his great victorie over *Amurath* the *Turk,*
and when the said King had compelled him to peace, 10
the most advantagious that ever was made for the
Christians, to breake his faith, and to provoke the *Turke*
to renew the warre.   And though the said King was
farre stronger in the field than ever ; yet he lost the
battaile with 30000. *Christians,* and his owne life.   But
I will stay my hand : For this first volume will not hold
the repetition of Gods judgements upon faith-breakers ;
bee it against *Infidels, Turkes,* or *Christians* of divers
Religions.   Lamentable it is, that the taking of oathes
now-a-daies, is rather made a matter of custome than of 20
conscience.

* *Psal.* 5. 6. *Wisd.* 1. 11.

§ IV.

[CONCERNING THE DEFENCE OF HARD PASSAGES.]

A digression concerning the defence of hard passages. Of things following the battaile of Granick.

THe winning of this passage did greatly encourage the *Macedonians*, and brought such terrour upon all those of the lesser *Asia*, as hee obtained all the Kingdomes thereof without a blow, some one or two Townes excepted. For in all invasions, where the Nations invaded have once beene beaten upon a great advantage of the place, as in defence of Rivers, Streights, and Mountaines, they will soone have perswaded themselves, that such an enemie, upon equall termes and even ground, can hardly be resisted. It was therfore *Machiavels* counsell, that he which resolveth to defend a passage, should with his ablest force oppose the Assailant. And to say truth, few Regions of any great circuit are so well fenced, that Armies, of such force as may be thought sufficient to conquer them, can be debarred all entrance, by the naturall difficultie of the waies. One passage or other is commonly left unguarded : if all be defended, then must the forces of the Country be distracted, and yet lightly, some one place will be found that is defended very weakely. How often have the *Alpes* given way to Armies, breaking into *Italie* ? Yea, where shall we finde that ever they kept out an invadour ? Yet they are such as (to speake briefly) afflict with all difficulties those that travaile over them ;

but they give no securitie to those that lie behinde them :
for they are of too large extent. The Townes of *Lumbardie*
perswaded themselves that they might enjoy their quiet,
when the Warlike Nation of the *Switzers* had undertaken
to hinder *Francis* the *French* King from descending into
the Duchie of *Milan* : but whilest these Patrons of
Milan, whom their owne dwelling in those Mountaines
had made fittest of all other for such a service, were
busied in custodie of the *Alpes* ; *Francis* appeared in
Lumbardie, to so much the greater terrour of the Inhabi- 10
tants, by how much the lesse they had expected his
arrivall. What shall we say of those Mountaines, which
locke up whole Regions in such sort, as they leave but
one Gate open ? The Streights, or (as they were called)
the Gates of *Taurus* in *Cilicia*, and those of *Thermopylæ*,
have seldome beene attempted, perhaps because they
were thought impregnable : but how seldome (if ever)
have they beene attempted in vaine ? *Xerxes*, and long
after him, the *Romans*, forced the entrance of *Thermopylæ* ;
Cyrus the younger, and after him *Alexander*, found the 20
Gates of *Cilicia* wide open ; how strongly soever they
had beene locked and barred, yet were those countries
open enough to a fleet that should enter on the back-
side. The defence of Rivers how hard a thing it is, wee
finde examples in all histories that beare good witnesse.
The deepest have many Foords; the swiftest and broadest
may bee passed by Boates, in case it be found a matter of
difficultie to make a Bridge. He that hath men enough
to defend all the length of his owne banke, hath also
enough to beate his enemie; and may therefore doe better 30

to let him come over, to his losse, than by striving in vaine to hinder the passage, as a matter tending to his owne disadvantage, fill the heads of his Souldiers with an opinion, that they are in ill case, having their meanes of safeguard taken from them, by the skill or valour of such as are too good for them. Certainly if a River were sufficient defence against an Armie, the Isle of *Mona*, now called *Anglesey*, which is divided from North-Wales by an arme of the Sea; had beene safe enough against the *Romans*, invading it under conduct of *Julius Agricola*. But he wanting, and not meaning to spend the time in making vessels to transport his forces, did assay the foords. Whereby hee so amazed the enemies attending for ships and such like provision by Sea, that surely beleeving nothing could bee hard or invincible to men, which came so minded to Warre, they humbly intreated for peace, and yeelded the Iland. Yet the *Britaines* were men stout enough; the *Persians* were very dastards.

It was therefore wisely done of *Alexander*, to passe the River of *Granick* in face of the enemie ; not marching higher to seeke an easier way, nor labouring to convey his men ouer it by some safer meanes. For having beaten them upon their owne ground, hee did thereby cut off no lesse of their reputation, than of their strength, leaving no hope of succour to the partakers and followers of such unable Protectors.

Soone after this victorie he recovered *Sardis*, *Ephesus*, the Cities of the *Trallians* and *Magnesia*, which were rendred unto him. The Inhabitants of which, with the people of the Countrie, he received with great grace,

suffering them to be governed by their owne lawes.
For hee observed it well ; *Novum Imperium inchoantibus*
utilis clementiæ fama ; It is commodious unto such as lay
the foundations of a new Soveraignetie to have the fame of
being mercifull. Hee then by *Parmenio* wanne *Miletus*,
and by force mastred *Halicarnasseus*, which, because it
resisted obstinately, hee razed to the ground. From thence
hee entred into *Caria*, where *Ada* the Queene, who had
beene cast out of all that shee held (except the Citie of
Alinda) by *Darius* his Lieutenants, presented her selfe
unto him, and adopted him her sonne and successor ; which
Alexander accepted in so gracious part as hee left the
whole Kingdome to her disposing. Hee then entred into
Lycia, and *Pamphilia*, and obtained all the Sea-coasts,
and subjecting unto him *Pisidia*, he directed himselfe
towards *Darius* (who was said to be advanced towards
him with a marvailous Armie) by the way of *Phrygia* :
For all the Province of *Asia* the lesse, bordering upon the
Sea, his first victorie laied under his feet.

While he gave order for the government and setling
of *Lycia*, and *Pamphylia*, he sent *Cleander* to raise
some new Companies in *Peloponnesus*, and marching
towards the North, he entred *Celenas*, seated on the River
Mæander, which was abandoned unto him, the Castle
only holding out, which also after fortie daies was given
up : for so long time he gave them to attend succour
from *Darius*. From *Celenas* he past on through *Phrygia*
towards the *Euxine* Sea, till he came to a Citie called
Gordium, the Regall-seate, in former times, of King *Midas*.
In this Citie it was that he found the *Gordian*-knot, which

when hee knew not how to undoe, hee cut it a-sunder
with his sword. For there was an ancient prophecie did
promise to him that could untie it, the Lordship of all
Asia ; whereupon *Alexander*, not respecting the manner
how, so it were done, assumed to himselfe the fulfilling
of the prophesie, by hewing it in peeces.

But before he turned from this part of *Asia* the lesse
towards the east, hee tooke care to cleare the Sea-coast on
his backe, and to thrust the *Persians* out of the Ilands of
Lesbos, Scio, and *Coos,* the charge whereof he committed
unto two of his Captaines, giving them such order as he
thought to be most convenient for that service ; and
delivering unto them fiftie talents to defray the charge ;
and withall out of his first spoile gotten, he sent threescore
Talents more to *Antipater* his Lieutenant in *Greece,* and
Macedon. From *Celenas* he removed to *Ancira,* now
called *Anguori,* standing on the same River of *Sangarius,*
which runneth through *Gordium* : there hee mustred his
Armie, and then entred *Paphlagonia,* whose people
submitted themselves unto him, and obtained freedome
of tribute : where he left *Catus* Governour with one
Regiment of *Macedonians* lately arrived.

Here he understood of the death of *Memnon, Darius*
Lieutenant, which heartned him greatly to passe on towards him, for of this only Captaine hee had more
respect than of all the multitude by *Darius* assembled,
and of all the Commanders hee had besides. For so much
hath the spirit of some one man excelled, as it hath
undertaken and effected the alteration of the greatest
States and Common-weales, the erection of Monarchies,

the conquest of Kingdomes and Empires, guided handfuls
of men against multitudes of equall bodily strength,
contrived victories beyond all hope and discourse of
reason, converted the fearefull passions of his owne
followers into magnanimitie, and the valour of his enemies
into cowardize; such spirits have beene stirred up in
sundrie Ages of the world, and in divers parts thereof, to
erect and cast downe againe, to establish and to destroy,
and to bring all things, Persons and States, to the same
certaine ends, which the infinite spirit of the *Universall*, 10
piercing, moving, and governing all thinges hath ordained.
Certainely the things that this King did were marvailous,
and would hardly have beene undertaken by any man else:
and though his Father had determined to have invaded
the lesser *Asia*, it is like enough that he would have
contented himselfe with some part thereof, and not have
discovered the River of *Indus*, as this man did. The
swift course of victorie, wherewith he ranne over so large
a portion of the World, in so short a space, may justly
be imputed unto this, That he was never encountred by 20
an equall spirit, concurring with equall power against
him. Hereby it came to passe that his actions being
limited by no greater opposition, than Desert places,
and the meere length of tedious journies could make,
were like the *Colossus* of *Rhodes*, not so much to bee
admired for the workemanship, though therein also
praise-worthie, as for the huge bulke. For certainely
the things performed by *Xenophon*, discover as brave
a spirit as *Alexanders*, and working no lesse exquisitely,
though the effects were lesse materiall, as were also the 30

forces and power of command, by which it wrought. But he that would finde the exact patterne of a noble Commander, must looke upon such as *Epaminondas,* that encountring worthie Captains, and those better followed than themselves, have by their singular vertue over-topped their valiant enemies, and still prevailed over those, that would not have yeelded one foot to any other. Such as these are doe seldome live to obtaine great Empires. For it is a worke of more labour and longer time, to master the equall forces of one hardie and well-ordered State, than to tread down and utterly subdue a multitude of servile Nations, compounding the bodie of a grosse unweldie Empire. Wherefore these *Parvo Potentes,* men that with little have done much upon enemies of like abilitie, are to be regarded as choise examples of worth; but great Conquerors, to bee rather admired for the substance of their actions, than the exquisite menaging : exactnesse and greatnesse concurring so seldome, that I can finde no instance of both in one, save only that brave *Roman Cæsar.*

§ V.

[OF GRIFFINS.

A discourse of Griffins and other fables, and of the great mountains of America.]

*T*Ostatus also gathereth a fantasticall opinion out of *Rabanus,* who makes *Ophir* to be a Countrie, whose mountaines of gold are kept by *Griffins* : which moun-

taines *Solinus* affirmeth to be in *Scythia Asiatica*, in
these wordes. *Nam cùm auro & gemmis affluant, Griphes
tenent universa, alites ferocissimæ, Arimaspi cum his dimi-
cant, &c.* For whereas these Countries abound in gold,
and rich stone[s], the Griffins defend the one and the other:
a kinde of Fowle the fiercest of all other; with which
Griffins a Nation of people called *Arimaspi* make warre.
These *Arimaspi* are said to have beene men with one eye
only, like unto the *Cyclopes* of *Sicilia* : of which *Cyclopes*
Herodotus and *Aristeus* make mention : and so doth *Lucan* 10
in his third Booke: and *Valerius Flaccus* * : and *D. Siculus* †
in the storie of *Alexander Macedon.* But (for mine owne
opinion) I beleeve none of them. And for these *Arimaspi*,
I take it that this name signifying *One-eyed* was first
given them by reason that they used to wear a vizard
of defence, with one sight in the middle to serve both
eyes; and not that they had by nature any such defect.
But *Solinus* borroweth these things out of *Plinie*, who
speakes of such a Nation in the extreme North, at a place
called *Gisolitron*, or the Cave of the Northeast winde. 20
For the rest, as all fables were commonly grounded upon
some true stories or other things done : so might these
tales of the *Griffins* receive this Morall. That if those
men which fight against so many dangerous passages for
gold, or other riches of this world, had their perfect
senses, and were not deprived of halfe their eye-sight
(at least of the eye of right reason and understanding)
they would content themselves with a quiet and moderate
estate ; and not subject themselves to famine, corrupt

* *Flaccus l. 6.*   † *Diod. Sicul. l. 16.*

aire, violent heate, and cold, and to all sorts of miserable diseases. And though this fable be fained in this place, yet if such a tale were told of some other places of the world, where wild beasts or Serpents defend mountaines of gold, it might be avowed. For there are in many places of the world, especially in *America,* many high and impassable mountaines which are very rich and full of gold, inhabited only with Tigers, Lyons, and other ravenous and cruell beasts : into which if any man ascend
10 (except his strength bee very great) hee shall bee sure to finde the same warre, which the *Arimaspi* make against the *Griffins* : not that the one or other had any sense of [the] gold, or seek to defend that mettall, but being disquieted, or made afraide of themselves or their young ones, they grow inraged and adventurous. In like sort it may be said that the *Alegartos,* (which the *Ægyptians* call the *Crocadyles*) defend those Pearles which lye in the Lakes of the Inland : for many times the poore *Indians* are eaten up by them, when they dive for the
20 pearle. And though the *Alegartos* know not the pearle, yet they finde savour in the flesh and bloud of the *Indians,* whom they devoure.

§ VI.

[OF LIBERTY.

*Of the slackness of courage engendered by want of
liberty among a people.*]

WE may justly wonder, that these Kingdomes of
Syria, *Media*, *Babylon*, and many other Nations,
(which the victorie of *Alexander* had over-runne, with so
hastie a course, as gave him not leisure to take any good view
of them) were so easily held not only by himselfe, but by
the Captaines of his Armie after him. The hot conten- 10
tions for superioritie betweene the King of *Israel*, and those
of *Damascus* ; betweene *Ægypt*, and *Babylon* ; *Babylon*,
and *Nineve* ; the *Persians*, and many Countries ; argue
a more manly temper, to have once beene in those
people ; which are now so patient of a forraigne yoke,
that like Sheepe or Oxen, they suffer themselves to be
distributed, fought for, wonne, lost, and againe recovered,
by contentious Masters ; as if they had no title to their
owne heads, but were borne to follow the fortune of the
Macedonians. This will appeare the more strange, if wee 20
shall consider, how the severall States of *Greece* (many of
which had never possessed so large Dominion, as might
cause their Spirits to swell beyond their abilitie) did
greedily embrace all occasions of libertie : and how these
proud Conquerours were glad to offer it, desiring to have
them rather friends than servants, for feare of further
inconvenience.

It must therefore be noted, that most of these Countries,

had alwaies beene subject unto the rule of Kings, or
pettie Lords; whom the *Babylonians* and *Persians* long
since had rooted out, and held them in such bondage,
that few of them knew any other Law, than the command
of forraigne Masters. This had utterly taken from them
all remembrance of home-borne Princes, and incorpor-
ated them into the great body of the *Persian* Empire:
so that wanting within themselves al soveraign power,
or high authoritie, the life and spirit of every Estate;
10 they lay as dead, and were bereaved of motion, when that
Kingdome fell, whereof they lately had beene members.

Why the *Persian Satrapæ*, or Princes of that Empire,
did not when *Darius* was taken from them, as the *Macedonian* Captaines, after the death of *Alexander*, strive to
lay hold upon those Provinces, which had many ages beene
subject unto them, and scarce foure yeares in quiet possession of their enemies; or why at least they contended
not (when the terrible name of that great Conquerour
did cease to affright them) to get their shares among his
20 followers, if not wholly to dispossesse them of their new
purchases: it is a question, wherin, who is not satisfied,
may finde no lesse reason to suspect the Historie, than
authoritie to confirme it. For wee seldome reade, that any
small Kingdome, prevailing against a farre greater, hath
made so entire a conquest, in the compasse of ten yeares,
as left unto the vanquished no hope of recoverie, nor
meanes to rebell; especially when such disorders, or
rather utter confusion hath ensued, by the fury of civill
warre among the Victors.

30 The cause why the *Macedonians* held so quietly the

Persian Empire, is well set down by *Macchiavell*; and concernes all other Kingdomes, that are subject unto the like forme of Governement : the summe whereof is this. Wheresoever the Prince doth hold all his Subjects under the condition of slaves; there is the conquest easie, and soone assured : Where ancient Nobilitie is had in due regard, there is it hard to winne all, and harder to keepe that which is wonne. Examples of this are the *Turkish* Empire, and the Kingdome of *France*. If any Invader should prevaile so farre upon *Turkie*, that the great 10 *Sultan* and his Children (for brethren hee useth not to suffer alive) were taken or slaine : the whole Empire would quickly be wonne, and easily kept, without any danger of rebellion. For the *Bassaes*, how great soever they may seeme, are meere slaves; neither is there in all that large Dominion, any one man, whose personall regard could get the people to follow him in such an attempt, wherein hope of private gaine, should not countervaile all apparent matter of feare. Contrariwise, in *France*, it were not enough for him that would make a 20 conquest, to get into his hands the King and his Children; though hee further got the better part of the Countrie, and were by farre the strongest in the field. For, besides the Princes of the Roiall bloud, there are in that Kingdome store of great men; who are mightie in their severall Countries, and having certaine Royalties and Principalities of their owne; are able to raise Warre, in all quarters of the Realme; whereunto the remembrance of their owne ancient Families, and long continued Nobilitie, will alwaies stirre up and inflame them, so 30

that untill every one peece were won, and every one (an endlesse worke) of the chiefe Nobilitie, brought under or destroyed, the victorie were not compleat, nor well assured. It is true, that such power of the Nobilitie, doth often-times make way for an Invader; to whom the discontentments of a few can easily make a faire entrance. But such assistants are not so easily kept, as they are gotten: for they looke to bee satisfied at full, in all their demands; and having what they would, they
10 soone returne to their old allegeance, upon condition to keepe what they have, unlesse they be daily hired with new rewards: wherein it is hard to please one man, without offending another as good as himselfe. The *Turke*, on the other side, needes not to feare any perill, that might arise from the discontented spirits of his principall men. The greatest mischiefe that any of them could worke against him, were the betraying of some frontier Towne, or the wilfull losse of a battaile: which done, the Traitor hath spent his sting, and must either
20 flie to the enemie, whereby he looseth all that he formerly did hold, or else, in hope of doing some further harme, he must adventure to excuse himselfe unto his Master, who seldome forgives the Captaine, that hath not striven by desperate valour, against misfortune. As for making head, or arming their followers against the great *Sultan*, and so joyning themselves unto any Invader; it is a matter not to be doubted: for none of them have any followers or dependants at all, other than such, as are subject unto them, by vertue of their Offices and
30 Commissions. Now as this base condition of the principall

men, doth leave unto them no meanes, whereby to oppose
themselves against the flourishing estate of their Prince;
so would it weaken both their power and their courage
in giving him assistance, if adversitie should make him
stand in neede of them. For there is scarce any one
among the *Turkes Bassaes* or provinciall Governours,
that knowes either from whence he was brought, or from
whom descended, nor any one among them, that by the
losse and utter ruine of the *Turkish* Empire, can loose
any foot of his proper inheritance, and it is the proper 10
inheritance of the subject, which is also a Kingdome
unto him, which makes him fight with an armed heart
against the Conquerer, who hath no other device painted
on his Ensigne, than the picture of slaverie.

As in the *Turkish* Empire, so was the *Persian*, voide of
libertie in the Subjects, and utterly destitute of other
Nobilitie, than such as depended upon meere favour of
the Prince. Some indeede there were of the Royall
bloud, and others, descended from the Princes that joyned
with *Darius*, the Sonne of *Hystaspes*, in oppressing the 20
Magi: these were men of reputation in *Persia*; but their
reputation consisted only in their Pedigree, and their
safetie in not medling with affaires of State, which made
them little esteemed. In what small account these *Persian*
Princes were held, it may appeare by this, that the Kings
Uncles, Cosen Germans, and Brethren, were called by the
Kings, *Their Slaves*, and so did stile themselves, in speaking
unto these great Monarchs. That upon every light
occasion of displeasure they were handled as Slaves; it
is easie to be discerned, in that example of crueltie, 30

practised by *Xerxes* upon his owne brother *Masistes*, which hath beene formerly noted, in place more convenient. As for the *Satrapæ*, or Governours of the Provinces, it is needlesse to cite examples, proving them to have beene meere slaves : it may suffice, that their heads were taken from them at the Kings will ; that is, at the will of those Women and Eunuches, by whom the King was governed.

To this want of Nobilitie in *Persia*, may be added the generall want of libertie convenient among the people : a matter no lesse availeable, in making easie and sure the conquest of a Nation, then is the cause assigned by *Machiavel*. For as *Æsope* his Asse, did not care to runne from the enemies, because it was not possible, that they should loade him with heavier burthens, than his Master caused him daily to beare : so the Nations, that endure the worst under their owne Princes, are not greatly fearfull of a forraigne yoke ; Nor will be hastie to shake it off, if by experience they finde it more light, then was that whereunto they had beene long accustomed. This was it that made the *Gascoignes* beare such faithfull affection, to the Kings of *England* ; for that they governed more mildly than the *French* : this enlarged the *Venetian* jurisdiction in *Lumbardie* ; for the Townes that they wanne, they wanne out of the hands of Tyrannous oppressours : and this did cause the *Macedonians*, with other Nations, that had beene subject unto the posteritie of *Alexanders* followers, to serve the *Romans* patiently, if not willingly ; for that by them they were eased of many burthens, which had beene imposed upon them by their owne Kings.

So that of this tamenesse, which we finde in those
that had beene subjects of the *Persian* Kings, the reasons
are apparent. Yet some of these there were, that could
not so easily be contained in good order by the *Macedonians* : for they had not indeede beene absolutely
conquered by the *Persian*. Such were the *Sogdians*,
Bactrians, and other Nations about the *Caspian* Sea.
Such also were the *Arabians* bordering upon *Syria* :
against whom *Antigonus* sent part of his Armie ; thinking
therewith to bring them under; or rather to get a rich 10
bootie. The Captaine that hee sent fell upon the
Nabathæans, at such time as they were busied in a great
Mart, wherin they traded with the more remote
Arabians, for *Myrrhe*, *Frankinsense*, and other such
commodities. All, or most of these rich wares, together
with five hundred talents of silver, and many prisoners,
the *Macedonians* laid hold upon : for their comming was
suddaine, and unexpected. But ere they could recover
Syria, the *Nabathæans* over-tooke them, and finding them
wearie with long marches, made such a slaughter, that of 20
foure thousand foot, and sixe hundred horse, only
fiftie horse escaped. To revenge this losse, *Demetrius*
was set out with a greater power : yet all in vaine ; for
he was not resisted by any Armie, but by the naturall
defence of a vaste Wildernesse, lack of water, and of all
things necessarie. Therefore he was glad to make peace
with them ; wherein hee lost not much honor : for they
craved it, and gave him presents. Returning from the
Nabathæans, hee viewed the Lake *Asphaltites*, whence
he conceived hope of great profit that might be raised, 30

by gathering the Sulphure. With this good husbandrie
of his sonne, *Antigonus* was well pleased; and appointed
men to the worke : but they were slaine by the *Arabians*,
and so that hope vanished.

These pettie enterprises, with the ill successe accom-
panying them, had much impaired the good advantage
against *Ptolomie* : when the newes of *Seleucus* his victories
in the high Countries, marred all together. For neither
was the losse of those great and wealthy Provinces,
10 a matter to be neglected; neither was it safe to transport
the warre into the parts beyond *Euphrates*, whereby *Syria*
and the lower *Asia* should have beene exposed, to the
danger of ill affected Neighbours. A middle course
was thought the best ; and *Demetrius*, with fifteene
thousand foot and three thousand horse, was sent against
Seleucus. These forces being sent away, *Antigonus* did
nothing: and his sonne did lesse. For *Seleucus* was then in
Media ; his Lieutenants about *Babylon* withdrew themselves from necessitie of fight ; some places they fortified
20 and kept ; *Demetrius* could hold nothing that he got,
without setting in Garrison more men than he could
spare, neither did hee get much ; and therefore was faine
to set out the braverie of his expedition, by burning and
spoiling the Countrie ; which he did thereby the more
alienate, and as it were acknowledge to belong unto his
enemie, who thenceforth held it as his owne assured.

Antigonus had laid upon his sonne a peremptorie commandement, to returne unto him at a time prefixed :
reasonably thinking (as may seeme) that in such an unset-
30 led state of things, either the Warre might bee ended,

by the furie of the first brunt ; or else it would bee vaine
to strive, against all difficulties likely to arise, where want
of necessaries should frustrate the valour, that by length
of time was like to become lesse terrible to the Enemie.
Demetrius therefore, leaving behinde him five thousand
foote, and a thousand horse, rather to make shew of continuing the warre, than to effect much, where himselfe,
with greater forces could doe little more than nothing,
forsooke the enterprise, and went back to his Father.

§ VII.

[A COMPARISON BETWEEN ROMAN AND ENGLISH SOLDIERS.]

That neither the Macedonian nor the Roman Souldier,
was of equall valour to the English.

I Shall not neede to speake of her other conquests :
it was easie to get more when shee had gotten all this.
It is not my purpose to disgrace the *Roman* valour (which
was very noble) or to blemish the reputation of so many
famous victories : I am not so idle. This I say ; that
among all their warres, I finde not any, wherein their
valour hath appeared, comparable to the *English*. If
my judgement seeme over-partiall ; our warres in *France*
may helpe to make it good.

First, therefore it is well knowne ; that *Rome* (or
perhaps all the world besides) had never any so brave
a Commander in warre, as *Julius Cæsar* : and that no
Roman armie was comparable unto that, which served

under the same *Cæsar*. Likewise, it is apparent, that
this gallant Armie, which had given faire proofe of the
Roman courage, in good performance of the *Helvetian*
warre, when it first entred into *Gaule*; was neverthelesse
utterly disheartened, when *Cæsar* led it against the
Germans. So that we may justly impute, all that was
extraordinarie in the valour of *Cæsars* men, to their
long exercise, under so good a Leader, in so great a warre.
Now let us in generall, compare with the deedes done by
these best of *Roman* Souldiers, in their principall service;
the things performed in the same Countrie, by our
common *English* Souldier, leavied in haste, from following
the Cart, or sitting on the shop-stall: so shall we see the
difference. Herein will we deale fairely, and beleeve
Cæsar, in relating the acts of the *Romans*: but will call
the *French* Historians to witnesse, what actions were
performed by the *English*. In *Cæsars* time, *France* was
inhabited by the *Gaules*, a stout people, but inferiour to
the *French*, by whom they were subdued; even when
the *Romans* gave them assistance. The Countrie of *Gaule*
was rent in sunder (as *Cæsar* witnesseth) into many
Lordships: some of which were governed by pettie
Kings, others by the multitude, none ordered in such
sort as might make it appliable to the nearest Neighbour.
The factions were many, and violent: not onely in generall
through the whole Countrie, but betweene the pettie
States, yea in every Citie, and almost in every house.
What greater advantage could a Conquerour desire? Yet
there was a greater; *Ariovistus*, with his *Germans*, had
over-runne the Countrie, and held much part of it in a

subjection, little different from meere slaverie: yea, so
often had the *Germans* prevailed in warre upon the *Gaules*,
that the *Gaules* (who had sometimes beene the better
Souldiers) did hold themselves no way equall to those
daily Invaders. Had *France* beene so prepared unto our
English Kings, *Rome* it selfe, by this time, and long ere this
time, would have beene ours. But when King *Edward* the
third beganne his warre upon *France*, hee found the whole
Countrie setled in obedince to one mightie King; a King
whose reputation abroad, was no lesse, than his puissance [10]
at home; under whose Ensigne, the King of *Bohemia*,
did serve in person ; at whose call, the *Genowayes*, and
other Neighbour States, were readie to take armes :
finally, a King, unto whom one * Prince gave away his
Dominion, for love ; † another sold away a goodly Citie
and Territorie for monie. The Countrie lying so open
to the *Roman*, and being so well fenced against the *English*;
it is note-worthie, not who prevailed most therein (for
it were meere vanitie, to match the *English* purchases,
with the *Roman* conquest) but whether of the two gave the [20]
greater proofe of militarie vertue therein. *Cæsar* himselfe
doth witnesse, that the *Gaules* complained of their owne
ignorance in the Art of warre, and that their owne hardi-
nesse was over-mastered, by the skill of their enemies.
Poore men, they admired the *Roman* Towers, and Engines
of batterie, raised and planted against their walls, as more
than humane workes. What greater wonder is it, that such
a people was beaten by the *Roman* ; than that the *Caribes*,
a naked people, but valiant, as any under the skie, are

* The Dolphin of Viennois.   † The King of Majorca.

commonly put to the worse, by small numbers of *Spaniards* ? Besides all this, we are to have regard, of the great difficultie that was found, in drawing all the *Gaules*, or any great part of them, to one head, that with joynt forces they might oppose their assailants : as also the much more difficultie, of holding them long together. For hereby it came to passe, that they were never able to make use of oportunitie : but sometimes compelled to stay for their fellowes ; and sometimes driven, to give 10 or take battaile, upon extreme disadvantages, for feare, lest their Companies should fall a-sunder : as indeede, upon any little disaster, they were readie to breake, and returne every one to the defence of his owne. All this, and (which was little lesse than all this) great oddes in weapon, gave to the *Romans*, the honour of many gallant victories. What such helpe ? or what other worldly helpe, than the golden mettall of their Souldiers, had our *English* Kings against the *French* ? Were not the *French* as well experienced in feats of Warre ? Yea, did they not 20 thinke themselves therein our superiours ? Were they not in armes, in horse, and in all provision, exceedingly beyond us ? Let us heare, what a *French* writer * saith, of the inequalitie that was betweene the *French* and *English*, when their King *John* was readie to give the on-set, upon the *Black Prince*, at the battaile of *Poitiers*.†
JOHN *had all advantages over* EDWARD, *both of number*,

* *John de Serres.*

† JEAN *avoit tout l'avantage par dessus* EDOUARD, *le numbre, la force, le lustre, le pays, le prejuge (qui n'est pas communement une consideration de peu d'importance aux affaires du monde) & avec soi l'elite de sa Cavallerie lors estimee la meilleure de tout son Royaume.*

force, shew, Countrie, and conceit (the which is commonly
a consideration of no small importance in worldly affaires)
and withall, the choise of all his horse-men (esteemed then
the best in Europe) with the greatest and wisest Captaines
of his whole Realme. And what could he wish more ?

I thinke, it would trouble a *Roman* antiquarie, to finde
the like example in their Histories ; the example, I say,
of a King, brought prisoner to *Rome*, by an Armie of
eight thousand, which he had surrounded with fortie
thousand, better appointed, and no lesse expert warriours. 10
This I am sure of ; that neither *Syphax* the *Numidian*,
followed by a rabble of halfe Scullions, as *Livie* rightly
tearmes them, nor those cowardly Kings *Perseus* and
Gentius, are worthie patternes. All that have read of
Cressie and *Agincourt*, will beare me witnesse, that I doe
not alleage the battaile of *Poitiers*, for lack of other, as
good examples of the *English* vertue : the proofe whereof
hath left many a hundred better marks, in all quarters
of *France*, than ever did the valour of the *Romans*. If
any man impute these victories of ours to the long Bow, 20
as carrying farther, piercing more strongly, and quicker
of discharge than the *French* Crosse-bow : my answer is
readie ; that in all these respects, it is also (being drawne
with a strong arme) superiour to the Musket ; yet is the
Musket a weapon of more use. The Gunne, and the
Crosse-bow, are of like force, when discharged by a Boy
or Woman, as when by a strong Man : weakenesse, or
sickenesse, or a sore finger, makes the long Bow unserviceable. More particularly, I say, that it was the custome
of our Ancestors, to shoot, for the most part, *point blanck* : 30

and so shall hee perceive, that will note the circumstances
of almost any one battaile. This takes away all objection :
for when two Armies are within the distance of a Butts
length, one flight of arrowes, or two at the most, can be
delivered, before they close. Neither is it in generall
true, that the long Bow reacheth farther, or that it
pierceth more strongly than the Crosse-bow : But this
is the rare effect, of an extraordinarie arme ; whereupon
can be grounded no common rule. If any man shall
10 aske, How then came it to passe, that the *English* wanne so
many great battailes, having no advantage to helpe him ?
I may, with best commendation of modestie, referre him
to the *French* Historian * : who relating the victorie of
our men at *Crevant*, where they passed a bridge, in face
of the enemie, useth these words : *The English comes with*
a conquering braverie, as he, that was accustomed to gaine
every where, without any stay : hee forceth our garde, placed
upon the bridge, to keepe the passage. Or I may cite
another place of the same Authour, where hee tells, how
20 the *Britons*, being invaded by *Charles* the eight, King
of *France*, thought it good policie, to apparell a thousand
and two hundred of their owne men in *English* Cassacks ;
hoping that the very sight of the *English* red Crosse,
would be enough to terrifie the *French*. But I will not
stand to borrow of the *French* Historians (all which, ex-
cepting *De Serres*, and *Paulus Æmylius*; report wonders
of our Nation) the proposition which first I undertooke
to maintaine ; *That the militarie vertue of the English,*
prevailing against all manner of difficulties, ought to be

* *John de Serres.*

preferred before that of the Romans, which was assisted
with all advantages that could be desired. If it be demanded;
why then did not our Kings finish the conquest, as
Cæsar had done ? my answere may bee (I hope without
offence) that our Kings were like to the race of the *Æacidæ*,
of whom the old Poet *Ennius* gave this note ; *Belli-*
potentes sunt magè quam sapientipotentes ; *They were more*
warlike than politique. Who so notes their proceedings,
may finde, that none of them went to worke like a Conquerour : save onely King *Henrie* the fift, the course of 10
whose victories, it pleased God to interrupt by his death.
But this question is the more easily answered, if another
be first made. Why did not the *Romans* attempt the
conquest of *Gaule*, before the time of *Cæsar* ? why not
after the *Macedonian* war ? why not after the third
Punick, or after the *Numantian* ? At all these times
they had good leisure : and then especially had they
both leisure, and fit oportunitie, when under the conduct
of *Marius*, they had newly vanquished the *Cimbri*, and *Teu-*
tones, by whom the Countrie of *Gaule* had beene piteously 20
wasted. Surely, the words of *Tullie* were true; that
with other Nations, the *Romans* fought for Dominion;
with the *Gaules*, for preservation of their owne safetie.

Therefore they attempted not the conquest of *Gaule*,
untill they were Lords of all other Countries, to them
knowne. We on the other side, held onely the one halfe
of our owne Iland ; the other halfe being inhabited by
a Nation (unlesse perhaps in wealth and numbers of men
somewhat inferiour) every way equall to our selves ;
a Nation, anciently & strongly allied to our enemies 30

the *French*, and in that regard, enemie to us. So that our danger lay both before and behinde us : and the greater danger at our backs ; where commonly we felt, alwaies we feared, a stronger invasion by land, than we could make upon *France*, transporting our forces over Sea.

It is usuall, with men, that have pleased themselves, in admiring the matters which they finde in ancient Histories ; to hold it a great injurie done to their judgment, if any take upon him, by way of comparison, to extoll the things of later ages. But I am well perswaded, that as the divided vertue of this our Iland, hath given more noble proofe of it selfe ; than under so worthie a Leader, that *Roman* Armie could doe, which afterwards could win *Rome*, and all her Empire, making *Cæsar* a *Monarch* ; so hereafter, by Gods blessing, who hath converted our greatest hindrance, into our greatest helpe, the enemie that shall dare to trie our forces, will finde cause to wish, that avoiding us, hee had rather encountred as great a puissance, as was that of the *Roman* Empire.

§ VIII.

[CONCERNING THE ART OF WAR AT SEA.

A discourse of Sea-fights in general and of the advantage of swift ships.]

TO prosecute this Warre, *Lucius Valerius* and *Titus Octacilius*, two new Consuls, are sent into *Sicil*. Whereupon, the Romans being Masters of the field, many inland Towns gave themselves unto them. On the contrarie, the *Carthaginians* keeping still the Lordship 10 of the Sea, many maritimate places became theirs. The *Romans* therefore, as well to secure their owne coasts, often invaded by the *African* fleets, as also to equall themselves in every kinde of warfare with their enemies, determine to make a fleet. And herein fortune favoured them with this accident, that being altogether ignorant in shipwrights-craft, a storme of winde thrust one of the *Carthaginian* Gallies, of five bankes, to the shore.

Now had the *Romans* a patterne, and by it they beganne to set up an hundred *Quinqueremes*, which were 20 Gallies, rowed by five on every banke, and twentie, of three on a banke : and while these were in preparing, they exercised their men in the feat of rowing. This they did after a strange fashion. They placed upon the Sea-sands many seates, in order of the bankes in Gallies, whereon they placed their water-men, and taught them to beate the sand with long poles, orderly, and as they

were directed by the Master, that so they might learne
the stroke of the Gallie, and how to mount and draw
their Oares. *16320*

When their fleet was finished, some rigging and other
implements excepted, *C. Cornelius*, one of the new Consulls
(for they changed every yeare) was made Admirall: who
being more in love with this new kinde of warfare, than
well advised, past over to *Messena* with seventeene Gallies,
leaving the rest to follow him. There he staied not,
but would needes row along the coast to *Lipara*, hoping
to doe some peece of service. *Hannibal*, a *Carthaginian*,
was at the same time Governour in *Panormus*; who being
advertised of this new Sea-mans arrivall, sent foorth one
Boodes, a Senatour of *Carthage*, with twentie Gallies, to
entertaine him. *Boodes*, falling upon the Consull una-
wares, tooke both him and the fleet he commanded.
When *Hannibal* received this good newes, together with
the *Roman* Gallies, and their Consull; he grew no lesse
foolish hardie than *Cornelius* had beene. For he, fancying
to himselfe to surprize the rest of the *Roman* fleet, on
their owne coast, ere they were yet in all points provided;
sought them out with a fleete of fiftie saile: wherewith
falling among them, he was well beaten, and, leaving the
greater number of his owne behinde him, made an hard
escape with the rest: for of one hundred and twentie
Gallies, the *Romans* under *Cornelius* had lost but seventeene, so as one hundred and three remained, which were
not easily beaten by fiftie.

The *Romans*, being advertised of *Cornelius* his overthrow, make haste to redeeme him, but give the charge of

their fleet to his Colleague, *Duilius*. *Duilius*, considering that the *Roman* vessels were heavie and slow, the *African* Gallies having the speede of them, devised a certaine engine in the prow of his Gallies, whereby they might fasten or grapple themselves with their enemies, when they were (as we call it) boord and boord, that is, when they brought the Gallies sides together. This done, the waightier ships had gotten the advantage, and the *Africans* lost it. For neither did their swiftnesse serve them, nor their Marriners craft; the Vessels, wherein 10 both Nations fought, being open: so that all was to be carried by the advantage of weapon, and valour of the men. Besides this, as the heavier Gallies were [accidentally] likely to crush and crack the sides of the lighter and weaker, so were they, by the reason of their breadth, more steadie; and those that best kept their feet, could also best use their hands. The example may be given between one of the long boates of his Majesties great ships, and a *London-barge*.

Certainely, he that will happily performe a fight at 20 Sea, must be skilfull in making choice of Vessels to fight in: he must beleeve, that there is more belonging to a good man of warre, upon the waters, than great during; and must know, that there is a great deale of difference, betweene fighting loose or at large, and grappling. The Gunnes of a slow ship pierce as well, and make as great holes, as those in a swift. To clap ships together, without consideration, belongs rather to a mad man, than to a man of warre: for by such an ignorant braverie was *Peter Strossie* lost at the *Azores*, when he fought against 30

the *Marquesse of Santa Cruz.* In like sort had the Lord *Charles Howard*, Admirall of *England*, beene lost in the yeere 1588. if he had not beene better advised, than a great many malignant fooles were, that found fault with his demeanour. The *Spaniards* had an Armie aboord them; and he had none: they had more ships than he had, and of higher building and charging; so that, had he intangled himselfe with those great and powerfull Vessels, he had greatly endangered this Kingdome of
10 *England.* For twentie men upon the defences, are equall to an hundred that boord and enter; whereas then, contrariwise, the *Spaniards* had an hundred, for twentie of ours, to defend themselves withall. But our Admirall knew his advantage, and held it: which had he not done, he had not beene worthie to have held his head. Here to speake in generall of Sea-fight (for particulars are fitter for private hands, than for the Presse) I say, That a fleete of twentie shippes, all good sailers, and good ships, have the advantage, on the open Sea, of an hundred
20 as good ships, and of slower sayling. For if the fleet of an hundred saile keepe themselves neare together, in a grosse squadron; the twentie ships, charging them upon any angle, shall force them to give ground, and to fall backe upon their owne next fellowes: of which so many as intangle, are made unserviceable, or lost. Force them they may easily, because the twentie ships, which give themselves scope, after they have given one broad side of Artillerie, by clapping into the winde, and staying, they may give them the other: and so the twentie ships
30 batter them in peeces with a perpetuall vollie; whereas

those, that fight in a troupe, have no roome to turne, and can alwaies use but one and the same beaten side. If the fleet of an hundred saile give themselves any distance, then shall the lesser fleet prevaile, either against those that are a-reare and hindmost, or against those, that by advantage of over-sailing their fellowes keepe the winde : and if upon a Lee-shore, the ships next the winde be constrained to fall back into their owne squadron, then it is all to nothing, that the whole fleet must suffer shipwrack, or render it selfe. That such advantage may be taken upon a fleet of unequall speede, it hath beene well enough conceived in old time ; as by that Oration of *Hermocrates,* in *Thucydides,** which he made to the *Syracusians,* when the *Athenians* invaded them, it may easily be observed.

Of the Art of Warre by Sea, I had written a Treatise, for the Lord HENRIE, *Prince of Wales* ; a subject, to my knowledge, never handled by any man, ancient or moderne : but God hath spared me the labour of finishing it, by his losse ; by the losse of that brave Prince ; of which, like an Eclypse of the Sunne, wee shall finde the effects hereafter. Impossible it is to equall wordes and sorrowes ; I will therefore leave him in the hands of God that hath him. *Curæ leves loquuntur, iugentes stupent.*

* *Thucyd. l. 6.*

§ IX.

[CONCERNING NAVAL TRANSPORT.]

The great advantages of a good fleet in warre, betweene
Nations divided by the Sea.

AN old example we have, of that great advantage of
transporting Armies by water, between *Canutus*,
and *Edmond Ironside*. For *Canutus*, when he had entred
the *Thames* with his Navie and Armie, and could not
prevaile against *London*, suddenly imbarqued ; and sailing
to the West, landed in *Dorset-shire*, so drawing *Edmond*
and his Armie thither. There finding ill entertainement,
he againe shipt his men, and entred the *Severne*, making
Edmond to march after him, to the succour of *Worcester-*
shire, by him greatly spoiled. But when he had *Edmond*
there, he sailed back againe to *London* : by meanes
whereof, he both wearied the King, and spoiled where he
pleased, ere succour could arrive. And this was not the
least helpe, which the *Netherlands* have had against the
Spaniards, in the defence of their libertie, that being
Masters of the Sea, they could passe their Armie from
place to place, unwearied, and entire, with all the Muni-
tion and Artillerie belonging unto it, in the tenth part of
the time, wherein their enemies have beene able to doe it.
Of this, an instance or two. The Count *Maurice* of
Nassau, now living, one of the greatest Captaines, and
of the worthiest Princes, that either the present or
preceding Ages have brought forth, in the yeare 1590.
carried his Armie by Sea, with fortie Canons, to *Breda* :

making countenance either to besiege *Boisleduc*, or *Ger-treuiden-Berg*; which the enemie (in prevention) filled with Souldiers, and victualls. But as soone as the winde served, he suddenly set saile, and arriving in the mouth of the *Meuze*, turned up the *Rhine*, and thence to *Yssel*, and sate downe before *Zutphen*. So before the *Spaniards* could march over land round about *Holland*, above fourescore mile, and over many great Rivers, with their Cannon and carriage, *Zutphen* was taken. Againe, when the *Spanish* Armie had over-come this wearisome march, 10 and were now farre from home, the Prince *Maurice*, making countenance to saile up the *Rhine*, changed his course in the night; and sailing downe the streame, he was set down before *Hulst* in *Brabant*, ere the *Spaniards* had knowledge what was become of him. So this Towne he also tooke, before the *Spanish* armie could returne. Lastly, the *Spanish* armie was no sooner arrived in *Brabant*, than the Prince *Maurice*, well attended by his good fleet, having fortified *Hulst*, set saile againe, and presented himselfe before *Nymegen* in *Gelders*, a Citie of notable 20 importance, and mastred it.

And to say the truth; it is impossible for any maritime Countrie, not having the coasts admirably fortified, to defend it selfe against a powerfull enemie, that is master of the Sea. Hereof I had rather, that *Spaine* than *England* should be an example. Let it therefore be sup-posed, that King *Philip* the second, had fully resolved to hinder Sir *John Norris* in the yeare 1589. from presenting *Don Antonio*, King of *Portugale*, before the gates of *Lysborne*; and that he would have kept off the 30

English, by power of his land-forces ; as being too weake
at Sea, through the great overthrow of his mightie *Armada*, by the fleet of Queene *Elizabeth*, in the yeare fore-
going. Surely, it had not beene hard for him, to prepare
an Armie, that should be able to resist our eleven thousand.
But where should this his Armie have beene bestowed ?
If about *Lysborne* ; then would it have beene easie unto
the *English*, to take, ransack, and burne the Towne of
Groine, and to waste the Countrie round about it. For
10 the great and threatning preparations, of the Earle of
Altemira, the Marquesse of *Seralba*, and others, did not
hinder them from performing all this. Neither did the
hastie leavie of eight thousand, under the Earle of
Andrada, serve to more effect, than the increase of honour
to Sir *John Norris*, and his Associates : considering, that
the *English* charged these, at *Puente de Burgos*, and passing
the great Bridge, behinde which they lay, that was
flanked with shot, and barricadoed at the further end,
routed them ; tooke their campe ; tooke their Generalls
20 standard with the Kings Armes, and pursued them over
all the Countrie, which they fired. If a roiall Armie, and
not (as this was) a Companie of private adventurers, had
thus begunne the warre in *Galicia* ; I thinke it would
have made the *Spaniards* to quit the guard of *Portugale*,
and make haste to the defence of their S^t. *Iago*, whose
Temple was not farre from the danger. But, had they
held their first resolution ; as knowing, that Sir *John
Norris* his maine intent was, to bring *Don Antonio*, with
an Armie, into his Kingdom, whither comming strong,
30 he expected to be readily and joyfully welcomed : could

they have hindred his landing in *Portugale* ? Did not he land at *Penicha*, and march over the Countrie to *Lysborne*, sixe daies journie ? Did not he (when all *Don Antonio* his promises failed) passe along by the River of *Lysborne* to *Cascaliz*, and there, having wonne the Fort, quietly imbarque his men, and depart ? But these, though no more than an handfull, yet were they *Englishmen*. Let us consider of the matter it selfe; what an other Nation might doe, even against *England*, in landing an Armie, by advantage of a fleet, if we had none. This question, *Whether an invading Armie may be resisted at their landing upon the coast of England, were there no fleet of ours at the Sea to impeach it* ; is alreadie handled by a learned Gentleman of our Nation, in his observations upon *Cæsars* Commentaries, that maintaines the affirmative. This he holds only upon supposition ; *in absence of our shipping*: and comparatively; as, that it is a more safe and easie course, to defend all the coast of *England*, than to suffer an enemie to land, and afterwards to fight with him. Surely I hold with him, that it is the best way, to keepe our enemie from treading upon our ground : wherein, if we faile, then must we seeke to make him wish, that he had staied at his owne home. In such a case, if it should happen, our judgements are to weigh many particular circumstances, that belong not unto this discourse. But making the question generall, and positive, *Whether England, without helpe of her fleet, be able to debarre an enemie from landing* ; I hold that it is unable so to doe : and therefore I thinke it most dangerous to make the adventure. For the incouragement of

a first victorie to an enemy, and the discouragement of
being beaten to the invaded, may draw after it a most
perilous consequence.

It is true, that the Marshall *Monluc*, in his Commentaries, doth greatly complaine, that by his wanting forces,
wherewith to have kept the frontier of *Guienne*, they of
the *Protestant* religion, after the battaile of *Moncounter*,
entred that Countrie, and gathered great strength and
reliefe thence; for if the King (saith he) would have
10 given me but reasonable meanes, *j'euse bien garde a*
Monsieur l'Admiral, de faire boire ses Chevaux en la
Garonne ; I would have kept the Admiral from watering
his horses in the River of Garonne. Monsieur de Langey,
on the contrarie side, preferres the not fighting upon
a frontier with an invading enemie, and commends the
delay; which course the Constable of *France* held,
against the Emperour *Charles*, when he invaded *Provence*.
Great difference I know there is, and a diverse consideration to be had, betweene such a Countrie as *France* is,
20 strengthned with many fortified places; and this of
ours, where our Rampars are but of the bodies of men.
And it was of invasions upon firme land, that these great
Captaines spake : whose entrances cannot be uncertaine.
But our question is, of an Armie to be transported over
Sea, and to be landed againe in an enemies Countrie, and
the place left to the choice of the Invader. Here-
unto I say, That such an Armie cannot be resisted
on the coast of *England*, without a fleet to impeach it; no, nor on the coast of *France*, or any other
30 Countrie : except every Creeke, Port, or sandie Bay,

had a powerfull Armie, in each of them, to make opposition.
For let his whole supposition be granted ; That *Kent*
is able to furnish twelve thousand foot, and that those
twelve thousand be laied in the three best landing places
within that Countie, to wit, three thousand at *Margat*,
three thousand at the *Nesse*, and sixe thousand at
Foulkston, that is somewhat equally distant from them
both ; as also that two of these troups (unlesse some
other order be thought more fit) be directed to strengthen
the third, when they shall see the enemies fleet to bend 10
towards it : I say, that notwithstanding this provision,
if the enemie, setting saile from the Isle of *Wight*, in the
first watch of the night, and towing their long boats at
their sternes, shall arrive by dawne of day at the
Nesse, and thrust their Armie on shore there ; it will be
hard for those three thousand that are at *Margat*, (twentie
and foure long miles from thence) to come time enough
to re-enforce their fellowes at the *Nesse*. Nay, how shall
they at *Foulkston* bee able to doe it, who are nearer by more
than halfe the way ? seeing that the enemie, at his first 20
arrivall, will either make his entrance by force, with
three or foure hundred shot of great Artillerie, and quickly
put the first three thousand, that were intrenched at the
Nesse, to runne ; or else give them so much to doe, that
they shall be glad to send for helpe to *Foulkston*; and perhaps to *Margat* : whereby those places will be left bare.
Now let us suppose, that all the twelve thousand *Kentish*
Souldiers arrive at the *Nesse*, ere the enemie can be readie
to disimbarque his Armie, so that he shall find it unsafe,
to land in the face of so many, prepared to withstand 30

him ; yet must we beleeve, that he will play the best of
his owne game; and (having libertie to goe which way he
list) under covert of the night, set saile towards the East,
where what shall hinder him to take ground, either at
Margat, the *Downes*, or elsewhere, before they at the
Nesse can be well aware of his departure ? Certainely,
there is nothing more easie than to doe it. Yea the like
may bee said of *Weymouth*, *Purbeck*, *Poole*, and of all
landing places on the South coast. For there is no man
10 ignorant, that ships, without putting themselves out of
breath, will easily out-runne the Souldiers that coast them.
Les Armees ne volent poynt en poste ; *Armies neither flye,
nor runne post*, saith a Marshall of *France*. And I know it
to be true, that a fleet of ships may be seene at Sunne-set,
and after it, at the *Lisard* ; yet by the next morning they
may recover *Portland*, whereas an Armie of foot shall not
bee able to march it in sixe daies. Againe, when those
troups, lodged on the Sea-shores, shall be forced to
runne from place to place in vaine, after a fleet of ships ;
20 they will at length sit downe in the mid-way, and leave
all at adventure. But say it were otherwise ; That the
invading enemie will offer to land in some such place,
where there shall be an Armie of ours readie to receive
him ; yet it cannot be doubted, but that when the choice
of all our trained bands, and the choice of our Commanders
and Captaines, shall be drawne together (as they were at
Tilburie in the yeare 1588) to attend the person of the
Prince, and for the defence of the Citie of *London* : they
that remaine to guard the coast, can be of no such force,
30 as to encounter an Armie like unto that, wherewith it

was intended that the Prince of *Parma* should have landed in *England*.

The Isle of *Tercera* hath taught us by experience, what to thinke in such a case. There are not many Ilands in the world, better fenced by nature, and strengthned by art : it being every where hard of accesse ; having no good harbour wherein to shelter a Navie of friends ; and upon every cove or watering place a Fort erected, to forbid the approch of an enemies boat. Yet when *Emanuel de Sylva*, and *Monsieur de Chattes*, that ₁₀ held it to the use of *Don Antonio*, with five or sixe thousand men, thought to have kept the *Marquesse of Santa Cruz*, from setting foot on ground therein ; the Marquesse having shewed himselfe in the Roade of *Angra*, did set saile, ere any was aware of it, and arrived at the *Port des Moles*, farre distant from thence ; where hee wanne a Fort, and landed, ere *Monsieur de Chattes*, running thither in vaine, could come to hinder him. The example of *Philip Strossie*, slaine the yeare before, without all regard of his worth, and of three hundred *French* prisoners ₂₀ murdered in cold bloud, had instructed *de Chattes* and his followers, what they might expect at that Marquesse his hands : Therefore it is not like, that they were slow in carrying reliefe to *Port des Moles*. Whether our *English* would bee perswaded to make such diligent haste, from *Margat* to the *Nesse*, and backe againe, it may bee doubted. Sure I am, that it were a greater march than all the length of *Tercera* ; whereof the *French-men* had not measured the one halfe, when they found themselves prevented by the more nimble ships of *Spaine*.   ₃₀

This may suffice to prove, that a strong Armie, in a good fleet, which neither foot, nor horse, is able to follow, cannot be denied to land where it list, in *England*, *France*, or elsewhere, unlesse it be hindered, encountred, and shuffled together, by a fleet of equall, or answerable strength.

The difficult landing of our *English*, at *Fayal*, in the yeare 1597. is alleaged against this : which example moves me no way to thinke, that a large coast may bee defended against a strong fleet. I landed those *English* in *Fayal*, my selfe, and therefore ought to take notice of this instance. For whereas I finde an action of mine cited, with omission of my name; I may, by a civill interpretation, thinke, that there was no purpose to defraud me of any honour ; but rather an opinion, that the enterprise was such, or so ill managed, as that no honour could be due unto it. There were indeede some which were in that voiage, who advised me not to undertake it : and I hearkned unto them, somewhat longer than was requisite, especially, whilest they desired me, to reserve the title of such an exploit (though it were not great) for a greater person. But when they began to tell me of difficultie : I gave them to understand, the same which I now maintaine, that it was more difficult to defend a coast, than to invade it. The truth is, that I could have landed my men with more ease than I did ; yea without finding any resistance, if I would have rowed to another place; yea even there where I landed, if I would have taken more companie to helpe me. But, without fearing any imputation of rash-nesse, I may say, that I had more regard of reputation, in

that businesse, than of safetie. For I thought it to belong
unto the honor of our *Prince* & *Nation*, that a few
Ilanders should not thinke any advantage great enough,
against a fleet set forth by *Q. Elizabeth*: and further, I was
unwilling, that some *Low-Countrie* Captaines, and others,
not of mine owne squadron, whose assistance I had
refused, should please themselves with a sweet conceipt
(though it would have beene short, when I had landed in
some other place) *That for want of their helpe I was driven
to turne taile*. Therefore I tooke with me none, but men 10
assured, Commanders of mine owne squadron, with some
of their followers, and a few other Gentlemen, voluntaries,
whom I could not refuse ; as, Sir *William Brooke*, Sir
William Harvey, Sir *Arthur Gorges*, Sir *John Skot*, Sir
Thomas Ridgeway, Sir *Henrie Thinne*, Sir *Charles Morgan*,
Sir *Walter Chute*, *Marcellus Throckmorton*, Captaine
Laurence Kemis, Captaine *William Morgan*, and others,
such as well understood themselves and the enemie : by
whose helpe, with Gods favour, I made good the enterprise
I undertooke. As for the *working of the Sea, the steepenesse* 20
of the Cliffes, and other troubles, that were not new to
us, we overcame them well enough. And these (notwithstanding) made five or sixe Companies of the enemies,
that sought to impeach our landing, abandon the wall,
whereon their Musketiers lay on the rest for us, and
wonne the place of them without any great losse. This
I could have done with lesse danger, so that it should not
have served for example of a rule, that failed even in
this example : but the reasons before alleaged, (together
with other reasons well knowne to some of the Gentlemen 30

above named, though more private, than to be here laid
downe) made me rather follow the way of braverie, and take
the shorter course; having it still in mine owne power
to fall off, when I should thinke it meet. It is easily said,
that *the Enemie was more than a Coward*; (which yet was
more than we knew) neither will I magnifie such a small
peece of service, by seeking to prove him better : whom
had I thought equall to mine owne followers, I would
otherwise have dealt with. But for so much as concernes
the Proposition in hand ; he that beheld this, may well
remember, that the same enemie troubled us more in our
march towards *Fayal*, than in our taking the shore; that
he sought how to stop us in place of his advantage; that
many of our men were slaine or hurt by him, among whom
Sir *Arthor Gorges* was shot in that march ; and that such,
as (thinking all danger to bee past, when wee had wonne
good footing) would needes follow us to the Towne, were
driven by him, to forsake the pace of a man of warre, and
betake themselves to an hastie trot.

For end of this digression, I hope that this question
shall never come to triall ; his Majesties many moveable
Forts will forbid the experience. And although the
English will no lesse disdaine, than any Nation under
heaven can doe, to be beaten upon their owne ground
or elsewhere by a forraigne enemie; yet to entertaine
those that shall assaile us, with their owne beefe in their
bellies, and before they eate of our *Kentish* Capons,
I take it to be the wisest way. To doe which, his Majestie,
after God, will imploy his good ships on the Sea, and not
trust to any intrenchment upon the shore.

§ X.

[OF THE FALLS OF EMPIRES.

*Concerning the instability of kingly estates and the
continuance of boundless ambition in mortal men.*]

BY this which we have alreadie set downe, is seene
the beginning and end of the three first Monarchies
of the world; whereof the Founders and Erectours
thought, that they could never have ended. That of
Rome which made the fourth, was also at this time
almost at the highest. We have left it flourishing in the 10
middle of the field; having rooted up, or cut down,
all that kept it from the eyes and admiration of the
world. But after some continuance, it shall begin to
lose the beauty it had; the stormes of ambition shal
beat her great boughes and branches one against another;
her leaves shall fall off, her limbes wither, and a rabble
of barbarous Nations enter the field, and cut her downe.

Now these great Kings, and conquering Nations, have
bin the subject of those ancient Histories, which have
beene preserved, and yet remaine among us; and withall 20
of so many tragicall Poets, as in the persons of powerfull
Princes, and other mightie men have complained against
Infidelitie, Time, Destinie, and most of all against the
Variable successe of worldly things, and Instabilitie of
Fortune. To these undertakings, the greatest Lords of
the world have beene stirred up, rather by the desire
of *Fame*, which ploweth up the Aire, and soweth in the

Winde; than by the affection of bearing rule, which
draweth after it so much vexation, and so many cares.
And that this is true, the good advice of *Cineas* to
Pyrrhus proves. And certainly, as Fame hath often
beene dangerous to the living, so is it to the dead of no
use at all; because separate from knowledge. Which
were it otherwise, and the extreame ill bargaine of buying
this lasting discourse, understood by them which are
dissolved; they themselves would then rather have
wished, to have stolen out of the world without noise;
than to be put in minde, that they have purchased the
report of their actions in the world, by rapine, oppression,
and crueltie, by giving in spoile the innocent and labouring soule to the idle and insolent, and by having emptied
the Cities of the world of their ancient Inhabitants, and
filled them againe with so many and so variable sorts of
sorrowes.

Since the fall of the *Roman* Empire (omitting that
of the *Germaines,* which had neither greatnesse nor
continuance) there hath beene no State fearefull in the
East, but that of the *Turke*; nor in the West any Prince
that hath spred his wings farre over his nest, but the
Spaniard; who since the time that *Ferdinand* expelled
the *Moores* out of *Granado,* have made many attempts
to make themselves Masters of all *Europe.* And it is
true, that by the treasures of both *Indies,* and by the
many Kingdomes which they possesse in *Europe,* they are
at this day the most powerfull. But as the *Turke* is now
counterpoised by the *Persian,* so in stead of so many
Millions as have beene spent by the *English, French,*

and *Netherlands* in a defensive war, and in diversions against them, it is easie to demonstrate, that with the charge of two hundred thousand pound continued but for two yeares or three at the most, they may not only be perswaded to live in peace, but all their swelling and overflowing streames may be brought backe into their naturall channels and old bankes. These two Nations, I say, are at this day the most eminent, and to be regarded; the one seeking to roote out the Christian Religion altogether, the other the truth and sincere profession thereof, the one to joyne all *Europe* to *Asia*, the other the rest of all *Europe* to *Spaine*.

For the rest, if we seeke a reason of the succession and continuance of this boundlesse ambition in mortall men, we may adde to that which hath been already said; That the Kings and Princes of the world have alwayes laid before them, the actions, but not the ends, of those great Ones which præceded them. They are alwayes transported with the glorie of the one, but they never minde the miserie of the other, till they finde the experience in themselves. They neglect the advice of God, while they enjoy life, or hope it; but they follow the counsell of Death, upon his first approach. It is he that puts into man all the wisdome of the world, without speaking a word; which God with all the words of his Law, promises, or threats, doth infuse. *Death* which hateth and destroyeth man, is beleeved; God which hath made him and loves him, is alwayes deferred. *I have considered* (saith Salomon) *all the workes that are under the Sunne, and behold, all is vanitie and vexation of spirit*:

but who beleeves it, till Death tells it us ? It was Death,
which opening the conscience of *Charles* the fift, made him
enjoyne his sonne *Philip* to restore *Navarre* ; and King
Francis the first of *France*, to command that justice
should be done upon the Murderers of the Protestants in
Merindol and *Cabrieres*, which till then he neglected.
It is therfore Death alone that can suddenly make man
to know himselfe. He tells the proud and insolent, that
they are but Abjects, and humbles them at the instant ;
10 makes them crie, complaine, and repent, yea, even to
hate their forepassed happinesse. He takes the account
of the rich, and proves him a begger ; a naked begger,
which hath interest in nothing, but in the gravell that
fills his mouth. He holds a Glasse before the eyes of
the most beautifull, and makes them see therein, their
deformitie and rottennesse ; and they acknowledge it.

O eloquent, just and mightie Death ! whom none
could advise, thou hast perswaded ; what none hath
dared, thou hast done ; and whom all the world hath
20 flattered, thou only hast cast out of the world and despised :
thou hast drawne together all the farre stretched greatnesse, all the pride, crueltie, and ambition of man, and
covered it all over with these two narrow words, *Hîc
iacet.*

Lastly, whereas this Booke, by the title it hath, calles
it selfe, The first part of the *Generall Historie* of the *World*,
implying a *Second*, and *Third* Volume ; which I also
intended, and have hewen out ; besides many other dis-
couragements, perswading my silence ; it hath pleased
30 GOD to take that glorious *Prince* out of the world, to

whom they were directed; whose unspeakeable and never
enough lamented losse, hath taught mee to say with JOB,
*Versa est in Luctum Cithara mea, & Organum meum in
vocem flentium.*

§ XI.

[THE BATTLE OF SALAMIS.]

[† 1] *How* THEMISTOCLES *the Athenian drew the Greekes to fight at Salamis.*

THe Athenians had, before the comming of *Xerxes*,
removed their wives and children into *Træzene*,
Ægina, and *Salamis*, not so highly prizing their houses,
and lands, as their freedome, and the common libertie
of *Greece*. Neverthelesse this great zeale, which the
Athenians did shew for the generall good of their Countrie,
was ill requited by the other *Greekes*, who with much
labour were hardly intreated to stay for them at *Salamis*,
whilest they removed the wives and children out of their
Citie. But when the Citie of *Athens* was taken, it was
presently resolved upon, that they should forsake the
Ile of *Salamis*, and with-draw the fleet to *Isthmus*: which
neck of land they did purpose to fortifie against the
Persians, and so to defend *Peloponnesus* by Land and Sea,
leaving the rest of *Greece*, as indefensible, to the furie
of the enemie. So should the Ilands of *Salamis* and
Ægina have beene abandoned, and the Families of the
Athenians (which were there bestowed as in places of

securitie) have beene given over into mercilesse bondage.
Against this resolution *Themistocles*, Admirall of the
Athenian Fleet, very strongly made opposition; but in
vaine. For the *Peloponnesians* were so possessed with
feare of loosing their owne, which they would not hazard,
that no perswasions could obtaine of them, to regard
the estate of their distressed friends, and Allies. Many
remonstrances *Themistocles* made unto them, to allure
them to abide the enemie at *Salamis*; As first in private
10 unto *Eurybiades* the *Lacedæmonian*, Admirall of the
whole fleet; That the self same feare which made them
forsake those coasts of *Greece*, upon which they then
anchored, would afterward (if it found no check at the
first) cause them also to dissever the fleet, and every one
of the Confederates to with-draw himselfe to the defence
of his owne Citie and estate: Then to the Councell of
Warre which *Eurybiades* upon this motion did call
together (forbearing to object what want of courage
might worke in them hereafter) he shewed that the fight
20 at *Isthmus* would be in an open Sea, whereas it was more
expedient for them, having the fewer ships, to determine
the matter in the straights; and that, besides the safeguard of *Ægina*, *Megara*, and *Salamis*, they should by
abiding, where they then were, sufficiently defend
Isthmus, which the *Barbarians* should not so much as
once looke upon, if the *Greekes* obtained victorie by Sea;
which they could not so well hope for else-where, as in
that present place which gave them so good advantage.
All this would not serve to retaine the *Peloponnesians*,
30 of whom one, unworthy of memorie, upbraided *Themis-*

tocles with the losse of *Athens*, blaming *Eurybiades* for suffering one to speake in the Councell, that had no Countrie of his owne to inhabite. A base and shamefull objection it was, to lay as a reproch that losse, which being voluntarily sustained for the common good, was in true estimation by so much the more honourable, by how much it was the greater. But this indignitie did exasperate *Themistocles*, and put into his mouth a reply so sharpe, as availed more than all his former perswasions. Hee told them all plainely, That the Athenians wanted not a fairer Citie, than any Nation of *Greece* could boast of; having well-neare two hundred good ships of Warre, the better part of the *Græcian* fleet, with which it was easie for them to transport their Families and substance into any part of the world, and settle themselves in a more secure habitation, leaving those to shift as well as they might, who in their extremitie had refused to stand by them. Herewithall he mentioned a Towne in *Italie* belonging of old to the State of *Athens*, of which Towne he said an Oracle had foretold, That the *Athenians* in processe of time should build it a-new, and there (quoth hee) will we plant our selves, leaving unto you a sorrowfull remembrance of my words, and of your own unthankfulnesse. The *Peloponnesians* hearing thus much, beganne to enter into better consideration of the *Athenians*, whose affaires depended not, as they well perceived, upon so weake termes, that they should be driven to crouch to others; but rather were such, as might inforce the rest to yeeld to them, and condescend even to the uttermost of their owne demands.

For the *Athenians*, when they first embraced that
Heroicall resolution of leaving their grounds and houses
to fire and ruine, if necessitie should inforce them so farre,
for the preservation of their libertie; did imploy the most
of their private wealth, and all the common treasure, in
building a great Navie. By these meanes they hoped
(which accordingly fell out) that no such calamitie
should befall them by land, as might not well be counterpoised by great advantages at Sea : Knowing well, that
10 a strong fleet would either procure victorie at home, or
a secure passage to any other Countrie. The other States
of *Greece* held it sufficient, if building a few new ships
they did somwhat amend their Navie. Whereby it came
to passe, that, had they beene vanquished, they could
not have expected any other fortune than either present
death, or perpetuall slaverie ; neither could they hope
to be victorious without the assistance of the *Athenians*,
whose forces by Sea did equall all theirs together; the
whole consisting of more than three hundred and foure-
20 score bottomes. Wherefore these *Peloponnesians* beginning to suspect their owne condition, which would
have stood upon desperate points, if the fleet of *Athens*
had forsaken them; were soone perswaded, by the greater
feare of such a bad event, to forget the lesser, which they
had conceived of the *Persians* : and laying a-side their
insolent braverie, they yeelded to that most profitable
counsaile of abiding at *Salamis*.

IN the meane season the Persians had entred into
consultation, whether it were convenient to offer
battaile to the *Greekes*, or no. The rest of the Captaines
giving such advice as they thought would best please
the King their Master, had soone agreed upon the fight :
but *Artemisia* Queene of *Halicarnassus*, who followed
Xerxes to this warre in person, was of contrarie opinion :
Her counsaile was, that the King him selfe directly should
march toward *Peloponnesus*, whereby it would come to
passe, that the *Greeke* Navie, (unable otherwise to continue long at *Salamis* for want of provision) should
presently be disseevered, and every one seeking to preserve
his owne Citie and goods, they should, being divided,
prove unable to resist him, who had wonne so farre upon
them when they held together. And as the profit will bee
great in forbearing to give battaile; so on the other side
the danger will bee more (said shee) which wee shall under-
goe, than any neede requireth us to adventure upon; and
the losse, in case it fall upon us, greater than the profit of
the victorie which we desire. For if we compell the
enemies to flie, it is more than they would have done, wee
sitting still : but if they, as better Sea-men than ours, put
us to the worst, the journey to *Peloponnesus* is utterly
dasht, and many that now declare for us, will soone revolt
unto the *Greekes*. *Mardonius*, whom *Xerxes* had sent

for that purpose to the fleet, related unto his Master
the common consent of the other Captaines, and withall
this disagreeing opinion of *Artemisia*. The King well
pleased with her advice, yet resolved upon following the
more generall, but farre-worse counsaile of the rest ;
which would questionlesse have beene the same which
Artemisia gave, had not feare and flatterie made all the
Captaines utter that as out of their owne judgement,
which they thought to be most conformable to their
Princes determination. So it was indeede that *Xerxes*
had entertained a vaine perswasion of much good, that his
owne presence upon the shore to behold the conflict,would
worke among the Souldiers. Therefore he incamped
upon the Sea-side, pitching his owne Tent on the mount
Ægalæus which is opposite unto the Ile of *Salamis*,
whence at ease hee might safely view all which might
happen in that action, having Scribes about him to write
downe the acts and behaviour of every Captaine. The
neere approch of the *Barbarians*, together with the
newes of that timorous diligence, which their Countri-
men shewed in fortifying the *Isthmus*, and of a *Persian*
Armie, marching a-pace thither, did now againe so
terrifie and amaze the *Peloponnesians*, that no intreatie,
nor contestation would suffice to hold them together.
For they thought it meere madnesse to fight for a Countrie
alreadie lost, when they rather should endevour to save that
which remained unconquered ; propounding chiefly to
themselves what miserie would befall them, if loosing the
victorie, they should be driven into *Salamis*, there to bee
shut up, and besieged round in a poore desolate Iland.

Hereupon they resolved forth-with to set saile for *Isthmus*: which had presently beene done, if the wisedome of *Themistocles* had not prevented it. For he perceiving what a violent feare had stopt up their eares against all good counsaile, did practise another course, and forth-with labour to prevent the execution of this unwholesome decree; not suffering the very houre of performance to finde him busie in wrangling alteration. As soon as the Councell brake up, hee dispatched secretly a trustie Gentleman to the *Persian* Captaines, informing them truely of the intended flight, and exhorting them to send part of their Navie about the Iland, which incompassing the *Greekes* might prevent their escape; giving them withall a false hope of his assistance. The *Persians* no sooner heard than beleeved these good newes, well knowing that the victorie was their owne assured, if the *Athenian* fleet joyned with them; which they might easily hope, considering what abilitie their Master had to recompence for so doing, both the Captaines with rich rewards, and the People with restitution of their Citie, and Territories. By these meanes it fell out, that when the *Greekes* very early in the morning were about to waigh Anchor, they found themselves inclosed round with *Persians*, who had laboured hard all night, sending many of their ships about the Ile of *Salamis*, to charge the enemie in reare, and landing many of their men in the Isle of *Psyttalea*, which lyeth over against *Salamis*, to save such of their owne, and kill such of the *Græcian* partie, as by any misfortune should be cast upon the shore. Thus did meere necessitie enforce the

Græcians to undertake the battaile in the Straights of
Salamis, where they obtained a memorable victorie,
stemming the formost of their enemies, and chasing the
rest, who falling foule one upon another, could neither
conveniently fight nor flie. I doe not finde any particular
occurrences in this great battaile to be much remarkeable.
Sure it is that the Scribes of *Xerxes* had a wearisome
taske of writing downe many disasters that befell the
Persian fleet, which ill acquitted it selfe that day, doing no
10 one peece of service worthie the presence of their King,
or the registring of his Notaries. As for the *Greekes*,
they might well seeme to have wrought out that victorie
with equall courage, were it not that the principall
honour of that day was ascribed to those of *Ægina*, and
to the *Athenians*, of whom it is recorded, That when the
Barbarians did flie towards *Phalerus*, where the Land-
Armie of *Xerxes* lay, the ships of *Ægina* having possessed
the Straights, did sinke or take them, whilest the *Athenians*
did valiantly give charge upon those that kept the Sea,
20 and made any countenance of resisting.

[† III]   *Of things following after the battaile of Salamis :
and of the flight of* Xerxes.

A Fter this victorie, the *Greekes* intending, by way of
scrutinie, to determine which of the Captaines had
best merited of them, in all this great service ; every
Captaine, being ambitious of that honour, did in the
first place write downe his owne name, but in the second
place, as best deserving next unto himselfe, almost
every Suffrage did concurre upon *Themistocles*. Thus

private affection yeelded unto vertue, as soone as her owne turne was served. The *Persian* King, as not amazed with this calamitie, beganne to make new preparation for continuance of warre ; but in such fashion, that they which were best acquainted with his temper, might easily discerne his faint heart, through his painted lookes. Especially *Mardonius*, Author of the warre, began to cast a warie eie upon his Master, fearing lest his counsaile should bee rewarded according to the event. Wherefore purposing rather to adventure his life in pursuit of the victorie, than to cast it away by under-going his Princes indignation ; he advised the King to leave unto him three hundred thousand men, with which forces he promised to reduce all *Greece* under the subjection of the *Persian* Scepter. Herewithall he forgot not to sooth *Xerxes* with many faire wordes ; telling him, that the cowardise of those *Ægyptians*, *Phœnicians*, and *Cilicians*, with others of the like mettall, nothing better than slaves, who had so ill behaved themselves in the late Sea-service, did not concerne his honour, who had alwaies beene victorious, and had alreadie subdued the better part of *Greece*, yea taken *Athens* it self, against which the Warre was principally intended. These words found very good acceptance in the Kings eare, who presently betooke himselfe to his journey homewards, making the more hast, for that he understood, how the *Greekes* had a purpose to saile to *Hellespont*, and there to breake downe his bridge, and intercept his passage. True it was that the *Greekes* had no such intent, but rather wished his hastie departure, knowing that he

would leave his Armie not so strong, as it should have beene, had he in person remained with it. And for this cause did *Eurybiades* give counsaile, that by no meanes they should attempt the breaking of that bridge, least necessitie should inforce the *Persians* to take courage, and rather to fight like men, than die like beasts. Wherefore *Themistocles* did, under pretence of friendship, send a false advertisment to this timorous Prince, advising him to convay himselfe into *Asia* with all speed, before his
10 bridge were dissolved: which counsaile *Xerxes* tooke very kindly, and hastily followed, as before is shewed. Whether it were so that he found the bridge whole, and thereby repassed into *Asia*; or whether it were torne in sunder by tempests, and he thereby driven to imbarke himselfe in some obscure vessell, it is not greatly materiall; though the *Greekes* did most willingly imbrace the later of these reports. Howsoever it were, this flight of his did well ease the Countrie; that was thereby disburdened of that huge throng of people, which, as Locusts, had
20 before over-whelmed it.

§ XII.

[EPAMINONDAS.]

The great battaile of Mantinæa. The honourable death of Epaminondas, *with his commendation.*

Epaminondas, considering that his Commission was almost now expired, and that his attempts of surprising *Sparta* and *Mantinæa* having failed, the impression of terrour which his name had wrought in the *Peloponnesians*, would soone vanish, unlesse by some notable act he should abate their courage in their first grouth, and leave some memorable character of his expedition ; resolved to give them battaile, whereby he reasonably hoped both to settle the doubtfull affections of his own Associates, and to leave the *Spartans* as weake in spirit and abilitie, as he found them, if not wholly to bring them into subjection. Having therefore warned his men to prepare for that battaile, wherein victorie 10 should be rewarded with Lordship of all *Greece* ; and finding the alacritie of his Souldiers to be such, as promised the accomplishment of his owne desire ; he made shew of declining the enemie, and intrenching himselfe in a place of more advantage, that so by taking from them all expectation of fighting that day, he might allay the heate of their valour, and afterward strike their senses with amazement, when hee should come upon them unexpected. This opinion deceived him not. For with verie much tumult, as in so great and sodaine a danger, the enemie 20 ranne to Armes, necessitie enforcing their resolution, and the consequence of that daies service urging them to doe as well as they might. The *Theban* Armie consisted of thirtie thousand foot, and three thousand horse ; the *Lacedæmonians* and their friends were short of this number, both in horse and in foot, by a third part. The *Mantinæans* (because the warre was in their Countrie) stood in the right wing, and with them the *Lacedæmonians* : the *Athenians* had the left wing, the *Achæans*, *Eleans*, and others of lesse account, filled the body of the Armie. 30

The *Thebans* stood in the left wing of their owne battaile, opposite to the *Lacedæmonians*, having by them the *Arcadians*; the *Eubœans*, *Locrians*, *Sicyonians*, *Messenians*, and *Thessalians* with others, compounding the maine battaile; the *Argives* held the right wing; the horse-men on each part were placed in the flancks, only a troupe of the *Eleans* were in reare. Before the footmen could joyne, the encounter of the horse on both sides was very rough, wherein finally the *Thebans* prevailed, notwith-
10 standing the valiant resistance of the *Athenians*: who not yeelding to the enemie either in courage or skill, were over-laied with numbers, and so beaten upon by *Thessalian* slings, that they were driven to forsake the place, and leave their infanterie naked. But this retrait was the lesse disgracefull, because they kept themselves together, and did not fall backe upon their owne foot-men; but finding the *Theban* horse to have given them over, and withall discovering some Companies of foot, which had beene sent about by *Epaminondas*, to charge
20 their battaile in the reare, they brake upon them, routed them, and hewed them all in peeces. In the meane season the battaile of the *Athenians* had not only to doe with the *Argives*, but was hardly pressed by the *Theban* Horse-men, in such wise that it beganne to open, and was readie to turne back, when the *Elean* squadron of Horse came up to the reliefe of it, and restored all on that part. With farre greater violence did the *Lacedæmonians* and *Thebans* meete, these contending for Dominion, the other for the maintenance of their ancient honour, so
30 that equall courage and equall losse on both sides made the

hope and appearance of victorie to either equally doubtfull: unlesse perhaps the *Lacedaemonians* being very firme abiders, might seeme the more likely to prevaile, as having borne the first brunt, and furie of the on-set, which was not hitherto remitted ; and being framed by Discipline, as it were by Nature, to excell in patience, whereof the *Thebans*, by practice of a few yeares, cannot bee thought to have gotten a habite so sure and generall. But *Epaminondas* perceiving the obstinate stiffenesse of the Enemies to bee such, as neither the badde successe of 10 their owne horse, nor all the force of the *Bœotian* Armie, could abate so farre, as to make them give one foote of ground ; taking a choise Companie of the most able men, whom he cast into the forme of a Wedge, or Diamond, by the advantage of that figure against a squadron, and by his owne exceeding vertue, accompanied with the great strength and resolution of them which followed him, did open their rancks, and cleave the whole battaile in despight of all resistance. Thus was the honour of that day won by the *Thebans*, who may justly 20 bee said to have carried the victorie, seeing that they remained Masters of the ground whereon the battaile was fought, having driven the Enemie to lodge farther off. For that which was alleaged by the *Athenians*, as a token that the victorie was partly theirs, the slaughter of those Mercenaries upon whom they lighted by chance in their owne flight, finding them behinde their Armie, and the retayning of their dead bodies ; it was a Ceremonie regardable only among the *Greekes*, and served meerely for ostentation, shewing that by the fight they had 30

obtayned somewhat, which the Enemie could not get
from them otherwise than by request. But the *Thebans*
arrived at the generall immediate end of battaile; none
daring to abide them in the field: whereof a manifest
confession is expressed from them, who forsake the place
which they had chosen or accepted, as indifferent for
triall of their abilitie and prowesse. This was the last
worke of the incomparable vertue of *Epaminondas*, who
being in the head of that Warlike troupe of men, which
10 broke the *Lacedæmonian* esquadron, and forced it to
give back in disaray, was furiously charged on the sodaine,
by a desperate Companie of the *Spartans*, who all at once
threw their Darts at him alone; whereby receiving
many wounds, hee neverthelesse with a singular courage
maintayned the fight, using against the Enemies many of
their Darts, which hee drew out of his owne bodie; till
at length by a *Spartan*, called *Anticrates*, hee received so
violent a stroke with a Dart, that the wood of it brake,
leaving the yron and a peece of the tronchion in his
20 brest. Hereupon hee sunke downe, and was soone con-
veighed out of the fight by his friends; having by his
fall somewhat animated the *Spartans* (who faine would
have got his bodie) but much more inflamed with
revengefull indignation, the *Thebans*, who raging at this
heavie mischance did with great slaughter compell their
disordered enemies to leave the field; though long they
followed not the chase, being wearied more with the
sadnesse of this disaster, than with all the travaile of the
day. *Epaminondas* being brought into his Tent, was told
30 by the Phisitians, That when the head of the Dart should

bee drawne out of his bodie, hee must needes die. Hearing
this, hee called for his shield, which to have lost was held
a great dishonour: It was brought unto him. Hee bad
them tell him which part had the victorie; answere was
made, that the *Bœotians* had wonne the field. Then said
hee, it is faire time for mee to die, and withall sent for
Iolidas, and *Diophantes*, two principall men of Warre,
that were both slaine; which being told him, He advised
the *Thebans* to make Peace, whilest with advantage
they might, for that they had none left that was able to 10
discharge the office of a Generall. Herewithall he willed
that the head of the weapon should be drawne out of
his bodie; comforting his friends that lamented his
death, and want of issue, by telling them, that the
victories of *Leuctra* and *Mantinæa* were two faire Daugh-
ters, in whom his memorie should live.

So died *Epaminondas*, the worthiest man that ever was
bred in that Nation of *Greece*, and hardly to bee matched
in any Age or Countrie: for hee equalled all others in the
severall vertues, which in each of them were singular. 20
His Justice, and Sinceritie, his Temperance, Wisedome,
and high Magnanimitie, were no way inferiour to his
Militarie vertue; in every part whereof hee so excelled,
that hee could not properly bee called a Warie, a Valiant,
a Politique, a Bountifull, or an Industrious, and a Provi-
dent Captaine; all these Titles, and many other, being
due unto him, which with his notable Discipline, and
good Conduct, made a perfect composition of an
Heroique Generall. Neither was his private Conversation
unanswerable to those high parts, which gave him praise 30

abroade. For hee was Grave, and yet very Affable and
Curteous; resolute in publique businesse, but in his
owne particular easie, and of much mildnesse; a lover
of his People, bearing with mens infirmities, wittie and
pleasant in speech, farre from insolence, Master of his
owne affections, and furnished with all qualities that might
winne and keepe love. To these Graces were added great
abilitie of bodie, much Eloquence, and very deepe
knowledge in all parts of Philosophie and Learning,
10 wherewith his minde being enlightened, rested not in
the sweetnesse of Contemplation, but brake forth into
such effects as gave unto *Thebes*, which had ever-more
beene an underling, a dreadfull reputation among all
people adjoyning, and the highest command in *Greece*.

§ XIII.

[CONCERNING THE PIRACY OF QUEEN TEUTA.

How the Illyrians infested the coast of Greece; and how
Queen Teuta gave her people free liberty
20 *to rob all sorts at sea.*]

THe *Illyrians* inhabited the Countrie, now called
Slavonia: a troublesome Nation, impatient of rest,
and continually making warre for gaine, without other
regard of friend or foe. They were invited by *Demetrius*
King of *Macedon*, to help the *Mydionians*, his friends,
that were besieged by the *Ætolians*, for that they
refused to be of their societie. Before the *Illyrian*

succours came, the *Mydionians* were so farre spent, that the
Ætolians contended about the bootie : the old Prætor,
or chiefe Magistrate of their Nation, who was going
out of his Office, clayming to have the honor of the
victorie, and the division of the spoile to be referred unto
him ; for that he had in a manner brought the siege to
an end, and wonne the Towne : others, that were in hope
to be chosen into the Office, contradicting this, and
desiring that old orders might be kept. It was a pretie
strife, and somewhat like to that of the *French* in later 10
ages, who thought upon dividing the prey, before they
had wonne the victories, which anon they lost, at *Poitiers*
and at *Agincourt*. The *Ætolians* wisely compounded the
difference, ordering it thus ; That the old, and the new
Prætor, should bee joyntly intitled in the victorie, and have
equall authoritie in distribution of the gettings. But the
Illyrians finished the strife much more elegantly, and
after another fashion. They arrived, and landed, ere
any was aware of them ; they fell upon the *Ætolians* ;
and though good resistance was made, yet got the victorie, 20
partly by force of their owne multitude, partly by helpe
of the *Mydionians*, that were not idle in their owne
businesse, but stoutly sallied out of the Towne. Many of
the *Ætolians* were slaine, more were taken, their Campe
and all their baggage was lost : the *Illyrians* tooke the
spoile, and went their way ; the *Mydionians* erected
a Trophie, inscribing the names, both of their old and
new Magistrate (for they also chose new Officers at the
same time) as the *Ætolians* had directed them by example.

The successe of this voiage, highly pleased *Agron* 30

King of the *Illyrians* : not only in regard of the monie,
wherewith *Demetrius* had hired his assistance ; or of the
bootie that was gotten ; but for that having vanquished
the stoutest of the *Greekes,* hee found it not uneasie, to
enrich himselfe by setting upon the lesse warlike. For
joy of this, he feasted, and dranke so immoderately, that
he fell into a *Pleurisie,* which in few daies ended his life.
His Kingdome, together with his great hopes, he left
unto *Teuta,* his wife.

10   *Teuta* gave her people free libertie, to robbe all Nations
at Sea, making no difference betweene friend and foe; as
if shee had beene sole Mistresse of the salt Waters. Shee
armed a fleet, and sent it into *Greece* : willing her Captaines, to make Warre where they found advantage,
without any further respect. These fell with the westerne
coast of *Peloponnesus* ; where they invaded the *Eleans,*
and *Messenians.* Afterwards they returned along by
Epirus, and staied at the Citie of *Phœnice,* to take in
victuailes and other necessaries. There lay in *Phœnice*
20 eight hundred *Gaules* ; that having beene Mercenaries
of the *Carthaginians,* went about to betray, first *Agrigen-*
tum, then *Eryx,* to the *Romans* ; but failing to doe
either, they neverthelesse revolted, and were for their
misdeedes disarmed, and sent to Sea by the *Romans,* yet
entertained by these *Epirots,* and trusted to lie in Garrison
within their Towne. The *Gaules* were soone growne
acquainted with the *Illyrians,* to whom they betraied
Phœnice ; which deserved none other, in trusting them.
All *Epirus* was presently in armes, and hastned to drive
30 out these unwelcome guests. But whilest the *Epirots*

lay before the Towne, there came newes into their Campe, of another *Illyrian* Armie, that was marching thitherward by Land, under one *Scerdilaïdas* ; whom Queene *Teuta* had sent to help his fellowes.   Upon this advertisement, a part of them is sent away towards *Antigonia*, to make good that Towne, and the streights adjoyning, by which these new commers must enter into their Countrie ; another part of them remaines at *Phœnice*, to continue the siege.   Neither the one, nor the other, sped well in their businesse.   For *Scerdilaïdas* found meanes to joyne 10 with his fellowes ; and they that were besieged within *Phœnice*, sallied out of the towne, and gave such an overthrow to the *Epirots*, as made them despaire of saving their Countrie, without great and speedie help from abroad. Wherefore Embassadours were sent to the *Achæans* and *Ætolians* : craving their help, with very pittifull tearmes of entreatie.   They obtained their suit ; neither was it long, before an Armie, sent by these two Nations, was readie in *Epirus*, to present battaile unto *Scerdilaïdas*. But *Scerdilaïdas* was called home, by letters from *Teuta* 20 the Queene, that signified a rebellion of some *Illyrians* against her : so that he had no minde to put his forces to hazzard, but offered composition; which was accepted. The agreement was, That the *Epirots* might ransome their Towne, and all their people that were prisoners ; and that the *Illyrians* should quietly depart, with all their bootie and slaves.   Having made this profitable and honourable bargaine ; the *Illyrians* returned into their own Countrie by Land, sending their bootie away by Sea.   30

At their comming home, they found no such great trouble, as that which they brought, or had occasioned in this voiage. For in fulfilling the commandement of their Queene, they had taken many *Italian* Merchants, whilest they lay at *Phœnice* ; and made them good prize. Hereof the complaints, made unto the *Roman* Senate, were so frequent, that Embassadours were sent to require of *Teuta*, that shee should abstaine from doing such injuries. These Embassadours found her very jolly ; both for the riches which her fleet had brought in ; and for that shee had, in short space, tamed her Rebells, and brought all to good order, save only the towne of *Issa*, which her forces held streightly besieged. Swelling with this prosperitie, shee could hardly affoord a good looke to the unmannerly *Romans*; that found fault with her doings ; and calling them by a true name, *Pyracie*, required amends. Yet when their speech was ended, shee vouchsafed to tell them, That injurie in publike shee would doe them none: as for private matters, no account was to be made of them ; neither was it the manner of Kings, to forbid their Subjects to get commoditie, how they best could, by Sea. But (said the yonger of the two Embassadours) we *Romanes* have a manner, and a very laudable one, to take revenge in publike, of those private wrongs, that are borne out by publike authoritie: therefore we shall teach you, God willing, to reforme your Kingly manners, and learne better of us. These words the Queene tooke so impatiently, that no revenge could satisfie her, but the death of him that had spoken them. Wherefore, without all regard of the common Law of Nations, shee caused him to be slaine : as if that had beene the way, to set her heart at rest ; which was indeede the meane, to disquiet and afflict it ever after.

The *Romans*, provoked by this outrage, prepare two great Armies ; the one by Sea, consisting of two hundred saile, commanded by *C. Fulvius* ; the other by Land, led by *A. Posthumus*. They trouble not themselves any more, with requiring satisfaction : for this injurie is of such nature, as must be requited with mortall warre. It is indeede contrarie to all humane Law, to use violence towards Embassadours : the reason and ground whereof, seemes to bee this ; that since without mediation, there would never be an end of warre and destruction, therefore it was equally received by all Nations, as a lesson taught by Nature, that Embassadours should passe freely, and in safetie, betweene enemies. Neverthelesse, as I take it, this generall Law is not without limitation. For if any King, or State, lay hold upon Embassadours sent by their enemies, not unto themselves, but unto some third, whom they should draw into the quarrell ; then it is as lawfull, to use violence to those Embassadours (thus imploied, to make the warre more terrible) as it is to kill the men of warre, and subjects, of an enemie. And so might the *Athenians* have answered it, when they slue the *Lacedæmonian* Embassadours, that were sent to *Xerxes*, to draw him into a warre upon the *Athenians*. Neither are those Embassadours, which practise against the person of that Prince, in whose Countries they reside, warranted by any Law whatsoever. For whereas the true Office of an Embassadour residing, is the maintenance of amitie ; if it be not lawfull for one Prince, to practise against the life of another, much lesse may an Embassadour doe it, without incurring justly the same danger of punishment, with other Traitors ; in which case, his place gives him no priviledge at all. But we will leave this dispute to the *Civilians* ; and goe on with the revenge, taken by the *Romanes*, for the slaughter of their Embassadour *Coruncanus*.

The *Illyrian* Queen was secure of the *Romans*, as if they would not dare to stirre against her. She was indeede in an errour ; that hath undone many of all sorts, greater and lesse than shee, both before and since : *Having more regard unto fame, than unto the substance of things.* The *Greekes* were at that time more famous than the *Romans* ; the *Ætolians* and *Epirots* had the name of the most warlike people in *Greece*; these had shee easily vanquished, and therefore thought, that with the *Romans* shee should be little troubled. Had she considered, that her whole Armie, which wrought such wonders in *Greece*, was not much greater, than of ten thousand men; and that never-thelesse, it prevailed as much, by oddes of number, as by valour, or skill in armes ; shee would have continued to use her advantage, against those that were of more fame than strength, with such good caution, that shee should not have needed to oppose her late-gotten reputation, against those that were more mightie than her selfe. But shee was a woman, and did what shee listed. Shee sent forth a greater fleet than before, under *Demetrius* of *Pharos* ; with the like ample commission, to take all that could bee gotten. This fleet divided it selfe ; and one

part of it fell with **Dyrrachium* ; the other, with *Corcyra*.
Dyrrachium was almost surprized by the *Illyrians* ; yet
was it rescued by the stout Citizens. In † *Corcyra* the
Illyrians landed; wasted the Isle; and besieged the Towne.
Hereupon the *Ætolians* and *Achæans* were called in
to helpe : who came, and were beaten in a fight at Sea ;
loosing, besides others of lesse note, *Marcus Carynensis*,
the first Prætor of *Achaia*, whom *Aratus* succeeded. The
Towne of *Corcyra*, dismaied with this overthrow, opened
the gates unto *Demetrius Pharius* ; who tooke possession 10
of it, with an *Illyrian* Garrison : sending the rest of his
forces to besiege *Dyrrachium*. In the meane season,
Teuta was angrie with her Captaine *Demetrius* : I know
not why ; but so, as he resolved to trie any other course,
rather than to trust her.

The *Romans* were even readie to put to Sea, though
uncertaine which way to take, when advertisement was
brought to *C. Fulvius* the Consull, of *Demetrius* his feare
and discontent. Likely it was, that such an occasion
might greatly helpe to advance the businesse in hand. 20
Wherefore the Consull sailed thither ; where hee found
the Towne of *Corcyra* so well prepared to his hand by
Demetrius, that it not only received him willingly, but
delivered into his power the *Illyrian* Garrison, and submitted it selfe unto the *Roman* protection.

After this good beginning, the Consull sailed along

---

* *Dyrrachium*, sometime called *Epidamnus*, and now *Durazzo*, seated
upon the *Adriatick* Sea, betweene the Ilands of *Pharos* and *Corcyra*.

† *Corcyra*, an Iland of the *Adriatick* Sea, not farre from *Durazzo* ;
called now *Corfu*, and in the possession of the *Venetians*.

the coast, to * *Apollonia*; accompanied with *Demetrius*, whom he used thenceforth as his counsailer and guide. To *Apollonia* came also *Posthumus*, the other Consull, with the Land-Armie, numbred at twentie thousand foot, and two thousand horse. Thence they hasten towards *Dyrrachium*, which the *Illyrians* had besieged; but upon newes of the *Roman* Armie, they disperse themselves. From thence the *Romans* enter *Illyria*, and take *Parthenia*; beat the *Illyrians* by Sea, take twentie
10 of their ships; and enforce the Queene *Teuta* to forsake the coast, and to cover her selfe in *Rison*, farre within the Land. In the end, part of the *Romans* haste them homeward, and leave the best places of *Illyria* in the hands of *Demetrius*; an other part staies behinde, and prosecutes the war, in such sort, that *Teuta* was forced to begge peace: which shee obtained upon miserable conditions; to wit, That shee should quit the better part of *Illyria*, and pay tribute for the rest; and from thenceforth, never send any of her ships of warre, towards the
20 coasts of *Greece*, beyond the Iland of *Lissa*: except it were some one or two vessels, unarmed, and by way of Trade.

After this *Illyrian* war, the *Romanes* sent Embassadours into divers parts of *Greece*, signifying their love to the Countrie, and how, for good will thereunto, they had made warre with good successe upon *Teuta*, and her people. They hoped belike, that some distressed Cities would take this occasion, to desire their patronage: which if it

* *Appollonia*, a Citie neare *Dyrrachium*, or *Durazzo*, upon the Sea-coast. *Pinetus* cals it *Sissopolis*.

hapned, they were wise enough to play their owne games. But no such matter fell out. The Embassadours were only rewarded with thankes; and a decree made at *Corinth,* That the *Romans* thenceforth might be partakers of the *Isthmian* pastimes. This was an idle courtesie, but well meant by the vaine *Greekes,* and therefore well taken by the *Romans* : who by this *Illyrian* Expedition got nothing in *Greece,* save a little acquaintance, that shall be more hereafter.

A REPORT

OF THE TRVTH OF

the fight about the Iles of
Açores, this laſt
Sommer.

BETVVIXT THE

Reuenge, one of her Maieſties
Shippes,

And an Armada of the King
of Spaine.

LONDON
Printed for william Ponſonbie.
1 5 9 1.

A report of the truth of the fight about
the Isles of Açores, this last summer, betwixt the Revenge, one of her Majesties Shippes, and an Armada of the king of Spaine.

BEcause the rumours are diversly spred, as well in Englande as in the lowe countries and els where, of this late encounter between her majesties ships and the Armada of *Spain*; and that the Spaniardes according to their usuall maner, fill the world with their vaine glorious vaunts, making great apparance of victories: when on the contrary, themselves are most commonly and shamefully beaten and dishonoured; therby hoping to possesse the ignorant multitude by anticipating and forerunning false reports: It is agreeable with all good reason, for manifestation of the truth to overcome falshood and untruth; that the beginning, continuance and successe of this late honourable encounter of Syr *Richard Grinvile*, and other her majesties Captaines, with the Armada of *Spaine*; should be truly set downe and published without parcialitie or false imaginations. And it is no marvell that the Spaniard should seeke by false and slandrous Pamphlets, advisoes and Letters, to cover their owne losse, and to derogate from others their due honours, especially in this fight beeing performed farre of: seeing they were not ashamed in the year 1588, when they purposed the invasion of this land, to publish in sundrie languages in print, great victories in wordes, which they pleaded to have obteined against this Realme; and spredde the same in a most false sort over all partes of *France, Italie*, and else where. When shortly after it was happily manifested in verie deed to all Nations, how their Navy which they termed invincible, consisting of 240. saile of ships, not onely of their own kingdom, but strengthened with the greatest Argosies, *Portugall* Caractes, Florentines and huge Hulkes of other countries: were by thirtie of her Majesties owne shippes of warre, and a few of our owne Marchants, by the wise, valiant, and most advantagious conduction of the L. *Charles Howard*, high Admirall of England, beaten and shuffeled togither; even from the Lizard in *Cornwall*: first to *Portland*, where they shamefully left *Don Pedro de Valdes*, with his mightie shippe: from *Portland* to *Cales*, where they lost *Hugo de Moncado*, with the Gallias of which he was Captain, and from *Cales*, driven with squibs from their anchors: were chased out of the sight of England, round about *Scotland* and *Ireland*. Where for the sympathie of their barbarous religion, hoping to finde succour and assistance: a great part of them were crusht against the rocks, and those other that landed, being verie manie in number, were notwithstanding broken, slaine, and taken, and so sent from village to village coupled in halters to be shipped into England. Where her Majestie of her Princely and invincible disposition, disdaining to put them to death, and scorning either to retaine or entertaine them: [they] were all sent backe againe to theire countries, to witnesse and recount the worthy achievements of their invincible and dreadfull Navy. Of which the number of souldiers, the fearefull burthen of their shippes, the commanders names of everie squadron, with all other their magasines of provisions, were put in print, as an Army and Navy unresistible, and disdaining prevention. With all which so great and terrible an ostentation, they did not in all their sailing rounde about England, so much as sinke or take one ship, Barke, Pinnes, or Cockbote of ours : or ever burnt so much as one sheepcote of this land. When 10 as on the contrarie, Syr *Francis Drake*, with only 800. souldiers not long before, landed in their Indies, and forced *Santiago*, *Santo Domingo*, *Cartagena*, and the Fortes of *Florida*.

And after that, Syr *John Norris* marched from *Peniche* in *Portugall*, with a handfull of souldiers, to the gates of *Lisbone*, being above 40. English miles. Where the Earle of *Essex* himselfe and other valiant Gentlemen, braved the Cittie of *Lisbone*, encamped at the verie gates ; from whence after many daies abode, finding 20 neither promised partie, nor provision to batter : made retrait by land, in despight of all their Garrisons, both of Horse and foote. In this sort I have a little digressed from my first purpose, only by the necessarie comparison of theirs and our actions : the one covetous of honour without vaunt or ostentation ; the other so greedy to purchase the opinion of their own affaires, and by false rumors to resist the blasts of their owne dishonors, as they wil not only not blush to spread all maner of un-truthes : but even for the least advantage, be it but for 30 the taking of one poore adventurer of the English, will celebrate the victorie with bonefiers in everie town, alwaies spending more in faggots, then the purchase was worth they obtained. When as we never yet thought it worth the consumption of two billets, when we have taken eight or ten of their Indian shippes at one time, and twentie of the Brasill fleet. Such is the difference betweene true valure, and ostentation: and betweene honourable actions, and frivolous vaineglorious vaunts. But now to returne to my first purpose.

The L. *Thomas Howard*, with sixe of her Majesties ships, sixe victualers of London, the barke Ralegh, and two or three Pinnasses riding at anchor nere unto Flores, one of the Westerlie Ilands of the Azores, the last of August in the after noone, had intelligence by one Captaine *Midleton*, of the approch of the Spanish Armada. Which *Midleton* being in a verie good Sailer, had kept them companie three daies before, of good purpose, both to discover their forces the more, as also to give advice to my L. *Thomas* of their approch. He had no sooner delivered the newes but the Fleet was in sight: manie of our shippes companies were on shore in the Iland; some providing balast for their ships; others filling of water and refreshing themselves from the land with such thinges as they coulde either for money, or by force recover. By reason whereof our ships being all pestered and romaging everie thing out of order, verie light for want of balast. And that which was most to our disadvantage, the one halfe part of the men of everie shippe sicke, and utterly unserviceable. For in the *Revenge* there

were nintie diseased : in the *Bonaventure*, not so many
in health as could handle her maine saile. For had not
twentie men beene taken out of a Barke of Sir *George
Caryes*, his being commanded to be sunke, and those
appointed to her, she had hardly ever recovered England.
The rest for the most part, were in little better state.
The names of her Majesties shippes were these as
followeth : the *Defiaunce*, which was Admirall, the
Revenge Viceadmirall, the *Bonaventure* commanded by
Captaine *Crosse*, the *Lion* by *George Fenner*, the *Foresight* 10
by M. *Thomas Vavisour*, and the *Crane* by *Duffeild*.
The *Foresight* and the *Crane* being but smal ships;
onely the other were of the middle size; the rest,
besid[e]s the Barke *Ralegh*, commanded by Captaine
Thin, were victualers, and of small force or none. The
Spanish fleete having shrouded their approch by reason
of the Iland ; were now so soone at hand, as our ships
had scarce time to waye their anchors, but some of them
were driven to let slippe their Cables and set sayle. Sir
Richard Grinvile was the last waied, to recover the men 20
that were upon the Iland, which otherwise had beene
lost. The L. *Thomas* with the rest verie hardly recovered
the winde, which Sir *Richard Grinvile* not being able
to do, was perswaded by the maister and others to cut
his maine saile, and cast about, and to trust to the sailing
of the shippe : for the squadron of *Sivil* were on his
wether bow. But Sir *Richard* utterly refused to turne
from the enimie, alledging that he would rather chose
to dye, then to dishonour him selfe, his countrie, and
her Majesties shippe, perswading his companie that he 30

would passe through the two Squadrons, in despight of
them : and enforce those of *Sivill* to give him way.
Which he performed upon diverse of the formost, who
as the Marriners terme it, sprang their luffe, and fell
under the lee of the *Revenge*. But the other course
had beene the better, and might right well have beene
answered in so great an impossibilitie of prevailing.
Notwithstanding out of the greatnesse of his minde, he
could not bee perswaded. In the meane while as hee
10 attended those which were nearest him, the great *San
Philip* being in the winde of him, and comming towards
him, becalmed his sailes in such sort, as the shippe could
neither way nor feele the helme : so huge and high
carged was the Spanish ship, being of a thousand and five
hundreth tuns. Who after laid the *Revenge* aboord. When
he was thus bereft of his sailes, the ships that wer under
his lee luffing up, also laid him aborde : of which the next
was the Admirall of the Biscaines, a verie mightie and
puysant shippe commanded by *Brittan Dona*. The said
20 *Philip* carried three tire of ordinance on a side, and eleven
peeces in everie tire. She shot eight forth right out of
her chase, besides those of her Sterne portes.

After the *Revenge* was intangled with this *Philip*,
foure other boorded her ; two on her larboord, and
two on her starboord. The fight thus beginning at
three of the clocke in the after noone, continued verie
terrible all that evening. But the great *San Philip*
having receyved the lower tire of the *Revenge*, discharged
with crossebarshot, shifted hir selfe with all diligence
30 from her sides, utterly misliking hir first entertainment.

Some say that the shippe foundred, but wee cannot report it for truth, unlesse wee were assured. The Spanish ships were filled with companies of souldiers, in some two hundred besides the Marriners; in some five, in others eight hundreth. In ours there were none at all, beside the Marriners, but the servants of the commanders and some fewe voluntarie Gentlemen only. After many enterchanged voleies of great ordinance and small shot, the Spaniards deliberated to enter the *Revenge*, and made divers attempts, hoping to force her by the multitudes 10 of their armed souldiers and Musketiers, but were still repulsed againe and againe, and at all times beaten backe, into their own shippes, or into the seas. In the beginning of the fight, the *George Noble* of *London*, having received some shot thorow her by the Armados, fell under the Lee of the *Revenge*, and asked Syr *Richard* what he would command him, being but one of the victulers and of small force : Syr *Richard* bidde him save himselfe, and leave him to his fortune. After the fight had thus without intermission, continued while the day lasted 20 and some houres of the night, many of our men were slaine and hurt, and one of the great Gallions of the Armada, and the Admirall of the Hulkes both sunke, and in many other of the Spanish ships great slaughter was made. Some write that sir *Richard* was verie dangerously hurt almost in the beginning of the fight, and laie speechlesse for a time ere he recovered. But two of the *Revenges* owne companie, brought home in a ship of Lime from the Ilandes, examined by some of the Lordes, and others : affirmed that he was never so 30

wounded as that hee forsooke the upper decke, til an
houre before midnight ; and then being shot into the
bodie with a Musket as hee was a dressing, was againe
shot into the head, and withall his Chirugion wounded
to death. This agreeth also with an examination taken
by Syr *Frances Godolphin*, of 4. other Marriners of the
same shippe being returned, which examination, the said
Syr *Frances* sent unto maister *William Killigrue*, of her
Majesties privie Chamber.

10   But to return to the fight, the Spanish ships which
attempted to board the *Revenge*, as they were wounded
and beaten of, so alwaies others came in their places,
she having never lesse then two mightie Gallions by
her sides, and aboard her. So that ere the morning, from
three of the clocke the day before, there had fifteene
severall Armados assailed her ; and all so ill approved
their entertainment, as they were by the breake of day,
far more willing to harken to a composition, then hastily
to make any more assaults or entries. But as the day
20 encreased, so our men decreased : and as the light grew
more and more, by so much more grew our discomforts.
For none appeared in sight but enemies, saving one small
ship called the *Pilgrim*, commanded by *Jacob Whiddon*,
who hovered all night to see the successe : but in the
mornyng bearing with the *Revenge*, was hunted like a hare
amongst many ravenous houndes, but escaped.

All the powder of the *Revenge* to the last barrell was
now spent, all her pikes broken, fortie of her best men
slaine, and the most part of the rest hurt. In the beginning
30 of the fight she had but one hundreth free from sicknes,

and fourescore and ten sicke, laid in hold upon the
Ballast. A small troupe to man such a ship, and a weake
Garrison to resist so mighty an Army. By those hundred
all was sustained, the voleis, bourdings, and entrings of
fifteene shippes of warre, besides those which beat her
at large. On the contrarie, the Spanish were alwaies
supplied with souldiers brought from everie squadron :
all maner of Armes and pouder at will. Unto ours there
remained no comfort at all, no hope, no supply either of
ships, men, or weapons ; the mastes all beaten over board, 10
all her tackle cut a sunder, her upper worke altogither
rased, and in effect evened shee was with the water,
but the verie foundation or bottom of a ship, nothing
being left over head either for flight or defence. Syr
Richard finding himselfe in this distresse, and unable
anie longer to make resistance, having endured in this
fifteene houres fight, the assault of fifteene severall
Armadoes, all by tornnes aboorde him, and by estimation
eight hundred shot of great artillerie, besides manie
assaults and entries. And that himselfe and the shippe 20
must needes be possessed by the enimie, who were now all
cast in a ring round about him ; The *Revenge* not able
to move one way or other, but as she was moved with the
waves and billow of the sea : commanded the maister
Gunner, whom he knew to be a most resolute man, to
split and sinke the shippe ; that thereby nothing might
remaine of glorie or victorie to the Spaniards : seeing
in so manie houres fight, and with so great a Navie they
were not able to take her, having had fifteene houres time,
fifteene thousand men, and fiftie and three saile of men 30

of warre to performe it withall. And perswaded the
companie, or as manie as he could induce, to yeelde
themselves unto God, and to the mercie of none els;
but as they had like valiant resolute men, repulsed so
manie enimes, they should not now shorten the honour
of their nation, by prolonging their owne lives for a few
houres, or a few daies. The maister Gunner readilie
condescended and divers others; but the Captaine and
the Maister were of an other opinion, and besought
10 Sir *Richard* to have care of them: alleaging that the
Spaniard would be as readie to entertaine a composition
as they were willing to offer the same: and that there
being diverse sufficient and valiant men yet living, and
whose woundes were not mortall, they might doe their
countrie and prince acceptable seruice hereafter. And
(that where Sir *Richard* had alleaged that the Spaniards
should neuer glorie to haue taken one shippe of her
Majesties, seeing that they had so long and so notably
defended them selves) they answered, that the shippe
20 had sixe foote water in hold, three shot under water
which were so weakly stopped, as with the first working
of the sea, she must needes sinke, and was besides so crusht
and brused, as she could never be removed out of the place.

And as the matter was thus in dispute, and Sir *Richard*
refusing to hearken to any of those reasons; the maister
of the *Revenge* (while the Captaine wan unto him the
greater party) was convoyde aborde the Generall *Don
Alfonso Bassan*. Who finding none over hastie to enter
the *Revenge* againe, doubting least S. *Richard* would have
30 blowne them up and himselfe, and perceiving by the

report of the maister of the *Revenge* his daungerous
disposition: yeelded that all their lives should bee saved,
the companie sent for England, and the better sorte to
pay such reasonable ransome as their estate would beare,
and in the meane season to be free from Gally or imprisonment. To this he so much the rather condescended as
well as I have saide, for feare of further losse and mischiefe
to them selves, as also for the desire hee had to recover
Sir *Richard Grinvile*; whom for his notable valure he
seemed greatly to honour and admire.   10

When this answere was returned, and that safetie of
life was promised, the common sort being now at the
end of their perill, the most drew backe from Sir *Richard*
and the maister Gunner, being no hard matter to diswade
men from death to life. The maister Gunner finding
him selfe and Sir *Richard* thus prevented and maistered
by the greater number, would have slaine himselfe with
a sword, had he not beene by force withheld and locked
into his Cabben. Then the Generall sent manie boates
abord the *Revenge*, and diverse of our men fearing Sir 20
Richards disposition, stole away aboord the Generall
and other shippes. Sir *Richard* thus overmatched, was
sent unto by *Alfonso Bassan* to remove out of the *Revenge*,
the shippe being marvellous unsaverie, filled with bloud
and bodies of deade, and wounded men like a slaughter
house. Sir *Richard* answered that he might do with
his bodie what he list, for he esteemed it not, and as he
was carried out of the shippe he swounded, and reviving
againe desired the companie to pray for him. The
Generall used Sir *Richard* with all humanitie, and left 30

nothing unattempted that tended to his recoverie, highly commending his valour and worthines, and greatly bewailed the daunger wherein he was, beeing unto them a rare spectacle, and a resolution sildome approved, to see one ship turne toward so many enemies, to endure the charge and boording of so many huge Armados, and to resist and repell the assaults and entries of so many souldiers. All which and more, is confirmed by a Spanish Captaine of the same Armada, and a present actor in the 10 fight, who being severed from the rest in a storm, was by the *Lyon* of London a small ship taken, and is now prisoner in London.

The generall commander of the Armada, was *Don Alphonso Bassan*, brother to the Marquesse of *Santa Cruce*. The Admirall of the *Biscaine* squadron, was *Britan Dona*. Of the squadron of *Sivill*, Marques of *Arumburch*. The Hulkes and Flybotes were commaunded by *Luis Cutino*. There were slaine and drowned in this fight, well neere two thousand of the enemies, and two 20 especiall commanders *Don Luis de sant John*, and *Don George de Prunaria de Mallaga*, as the Spanish Captain confesseth, besides divers others of speciall account, wherof as yet report is not made.

The Admirall of the Hulkes and the Ascension of *Sivill*, were both suncke by the side of the *Revenge*; one other recovered the rode of Saint *Michels*, and suncke also there; a fourth ranne her selfe with the shore to save her men. Syr *Richard* died as it is said, the second or third day aboard the Generall, and was by them 30 greatly bewailed. What became of his bodie, whether it were buried in the sea or on the lande wee know not : the comfort that remaineth to his friendes is, that he hath ended his life honourably in respect of the reputation wonne to his nation and country, and of the same to his posteritie, and that being dead, he hath not outlived his owne honour.

For the rest of her Majesties ships that entred not so far into the fight as the *Revenge*, the reasons and causes were these. There were of them but six in all, wherof two but smal ships ; the *Revenge* ingaged past 10 recoverie : The Iland of *Flores* was on the one side, 53. saile of the Spanish, divided into squadrons on the other, all as full filled with soldiers as they could containe. Almost the one halfe of our men sicke and not able to serve : the ships growne foule, unroomaged, and scarcely able to beare anie saile for want of balast, having beene sixe moneths at the sea before. If al the rest had entred, all had been lost. For the verie hugenes of the Spanish fleet, if no other violence had been offred, would have crusht them between them into shivers. Of which the 20 dishonour and losse to the Queene had been far greater then the spoile or harme that the enemy could any way have received. Notwithstanding it is verie true, that the Lord *Thomas* would have entred betweene the squadrons, but the rest wold not condescend ; and the maister of his owne ship offred to leape into the sea, rather then to conduct that her Majesties ship and the rest to be a praie to the enemy, where there was no hope nor possibilitie either of defence or victorie. Which also in my opinion had il sorted or answered the discretion and trust of 30

a Generall, to commit himselfe and his charge to an assured destruction, without hope or any likelihood of prevailing : therby to diminish the strength of her Majesties Navy, and to enrich the pride and glorie of the enemie. The Foresight of the Queenes commanded by M. *Th. Vavisor*, performed a verie great fight, and stayd two houres as neere the *Revenge* as the wether wold permit him, not forsaking the fight, till hee was like to be encompassed by the squadrons, and with great
10 difficultie cleared himselfe. The rest gave divers voleies of shot, and entred as far as the place permitted and their own necessities, to keep the weather gage of the enemy, untill they were parted by night. A fewe daies after the fight was ended, and the English prisoners dispersed into the Spanish and Indy ships, there arose so great a storme from the West and Northwest, that all the fleet was dispersed, as well the Indian fleet which were then come unto them as the rest of the Armada that attended their arrivall, of which 14. saile togither with the *Revenge*,
20 and in her 200. Spaniards, were cast away upon the Isle of S. *Michaels*. So it pleased them to honor the buriall of that renowned ship the *Revenge*, not suffring her to perish alone, for the great honour she achieved in her life time. On the rest of the Ilandes there were cast away in this storme, 15. or 16. more of the ships of war ; and of a hundred and odde saile of the Indie fleet, expected this yeere in *Spaine*, what in this tempest, and what before in the bay of *Mexico*, and about the *Bermudas* there were 70. and odde consumed and lost,
30 with those taken by our ships of London, besides one verie

rich *Indian* shippe, which set her selfe on fire, beeing
boorded by the Pilgrim, and five other taken by Maister
Wats his ships of London, between the *Havana* and
Cape S. *Antonio*. The 4. of this month of November,
we received letters from the *Tercera*, affirming that there
are 3000. bodies of men remaining in that Iland, saved
out of the perished ships : and that by the Spaniards
own confession, there are 10000. cast away in this storm,
besides those that are perished betweene the Ilands
and the maine. Thus it hath pleased God to fight for 10
us, and to defend the justice of our cause, against the
ambicious and bloudy pretenses of the Spaniard, who
seeking to devour all nations, are themselves devoured.
A manifest testimonie how injust and displeasing, their
attempts are in the sight of God, who hath pleased to
witnes by the successe of their affaires, his mislike of their
bloudy and injurious designes, purposed and practised
against all Christian Princes, over whom they seeke
unlawfull and ungodly rule and Empery.

One day or two before this wrack hapned to the 20
spanish fleet, when as some of our prisoners desired to
be set on shore upon the Ilands, hoping to be from
thence transported into England, which libertie was
formerly by the Generall promised : One *Morice Fitz
John*, sonne of old *John* of *Desmond* a notable traitor,
cousen german to the late Earle of *Desmond*, was sent
to the English from ship to ship, to persuade them to
serve the King of *Spaine*. The arguments he used to
induce them, were these. The increase of pay which
he promised to bee trebled : advancement to the better 30

sort : and the exercise of the true Catholicke religion, and safetie of their soules to all. For the first, even the beggerly and unnaturall behaviour of those English and Irish rebels, that served the King in that present action, was sufficient to answere that first argument of rich paie. For so poore and beggerly they were, as for want of apparel they stripped their poore country men prisoners out of their ragged garments, worne to nothing by six months service, and spared not to despoile them even of their
10 bloudie shirts, from their wounded bodies, and the very shooes from their feete ; A notable testimonie of their rich entertainment and great wages. The second reason was hope of advancement if they served well, and would continue faithfull to the King. But what man can be so blockishly ignorant ever to expect place or honour from a forraine king, having no other argument or perswasion then his owne disloyaltie ; to bee unnaturall to his owne countrie that bredde him ; to his parents that begat him, and rebellious to his true prince, to whose
20 obedience he is bound by othe, by nature, and by religion. No, they are onely assured to be imployed in all desperate enterprises, to be held in scorne and disdaine ever among those whom they serve. And that ever traitor was either trusted or advanced I could never yet reade, neither can I at this time remember any example. And no man could have lesse becommed the place of an Orator for such a purpose, then this *Morice* of *Desmond*. For the Earle his cosen being one of the greatest subjects in that kingdom of *Ireland*, having almost whole contries in his
30 possession ; so many goodly manners, Castles, and

Lordships; the Count Palatine of *Kerry*, five hundred gentlemen of his owne name and familie to follow him, besides others. All which he possessed in peace for three or foure hundred yeares : was in lesse then three yeares after his adhering to the Spaniards and rebellion, beaten from all his holdes, not so many as ten gentlemen of his name left living, him selfe taken and beheaded by a souldiour of his owne nation, and his land given by a Parlament to her Ma[j]estie, and possessed by the English. His other Cosen Sir *John* of *Desmond* taken by M. *John* 10 *Zouch*, and his body hanged over the gates of his native citie to bee devoured by Ravens : the third brother Sir *James* hanged, drawne, and quartered in the same place. If he had withall vaunted of this successe of his owne house, no doubt the argument woulde have moved much, and wrought great effect ; which because he for that present forgot, I thought it good to remember in his behalfe. For matter of religion it would require a particuler volume, if I should set downe how irreligiously they cover their greedy and ambicious pretences, 20 with that vayle of pietie. But sure I am, that there is no kingdom or common wealth in all Europe, but if they bee reformed, they then invade it for religion sake : if it be, as they terme Catholike, they pretende title ; as if the Kinges of *Castile* were the naturall heires of all the worlde : and so betweene both, no kingdom is unsought. Where they dare not with their owne forces to invade, they basely entertaine the traitors and vacabondes of all nations ; seeking by those and by their runnagate *Jesuits* to win partes, and have by that meane 30 ruined many Noble houses and others in this land, and have extinguished both their lives and families. What good, honour, or fortune ever man yet by them achived, is yet unheard of, or unwritten. And if our English Papistes do but looke into *Portugall*, against whom they have no pretence of religion, how the Nobilitie are put to death, imprisoned, their rich men made a pray, and all sortes of people captived; they shall find that the obedience even of the Turke is easie and a libertie, in respect of the slaverie and tyrannie of *Spaine*. What they have done in *Sicill*, in *Naples*, *Millayne*, and in the low countries; who hath there beene spared for religion at all? And it commeth to my remembrance of a certaine Burger of *Antwerpe*, whose house being entred by a companie of Spanish souldiers, when they first sacked the Citie, hee besought them to spare him and his goodes, being a good Catholike, and one of their own partie and faction. The Spaniardes answered, that they knew him to be of a good conscience for him selfe, but his money, plate, jewels, and goodes were all heretical, and therfore good prize. So they abused and tormented the foolish Flemming, who hoped that an *Agnus Dei* had beene a sufficient Target against all force of that holie and charitable nation. Neither have they at any time as they protest invaded the kingdomes of the *Indies* and *Peru*, and els where, but onely led thereunto, rather, to reduce the people to Christianitie, then for either golde or emperie. When as in one onely Iland called *Hispaniola*, they have wasted thirtie hundred thousand of the naturall people, besides manie millions

els in other places of the *Indies* : a poore and harmelesse
people created of God, and might have beene won to
his knowledge, as many of them were, and almost as
manie as ever were perswaded thereunto. The Storie
whereof is at large written by a Bishop of their owne
nation called *Bartholome de las Casas*, and translated into
English and manie other languages, intituled *The Spanish
cruelties*. Who would therefore repose trust in such
a nation of ravinous straungers, and especially in those
Spaniardes which more greedily thirst after English 10
bloud, then after the lives of anie other people of Europe ;
for the manie overthrowes and dishonours they have
received at our handes, whose weaknesse we have
discovered to the world, and whose forces at home,
abroad, in *Europe*, in *India*, by sea and land ; we have
even with handfulles of men and shippes, overthrowne
and dishonoured. Let not therefore anie English man of
what religion soever, have other opinion of the Spaniards,
but that those whom hee seeketh to winne of our nation,
hee esteemeth base and traiterous, unworthie persons, 20
or unconstant fooles : and that he useth his pretence of
religion, for no other purpose, but to bewitch us from
the obedience of our naturall prince ; thereby hoping
in time to bring us to slaverie and subjection, and then
none shall be unto them so odious, and disdained as the
traitours themselves, who have solde their countrie to
a straunger, and forsaken their faith and obedience
contrarie to nature or religion ; and contrarie to that
humane and generall honour, not onely of Christians,
but of heathen and irreligious nations, who have alwaies 30

sustained what labour soever, and embraced even death it selfe, for their countrie, prince or common-wealth. To conclude, it hath ever to this day pleased God, to prosper and defend her Majestie, to breake the purposes of malicious enimies, of foresworne traitours, and of injust practises and invasions. She hath ever beene honoured of the worthiest Kinges, served by faithfull subjects, and shall by the favour of God, resist, repell, and confound all whatsoever attempts against her sacred 10 Person or kingdome. In the meane time, let the Spaniard and traitour vaunt of their successe ; and we her true and obedient vassalles guided by the shining light of her vertues, shall alwaies love her, serve her, and obey her to the end of our lives.

F I N I S.

A particuler note of the Indian fleet, expected to have come into Spaine this present yere of 1591. with the number of ships that are perished of the same: according to the examination of certaine Spanyards, lately taken and brought into England by the shippes of London.

THe fleet of *Nova Hispania*, at their first gathering togither and setting foorth, were 52. sailes. The Admiral was of 600. tuns, and the Vice Admirall of the same burthen. Foure or five of the ships were of 900. and 1000. tunnes a peece, some 500. and 400. and the least of 200. tunnes. Of this fleet 19. were cast away, and in them 2600. men by estimation, which was done along the coast of *Nova Hispania*, so that of the same fleet, there came to the *Havana*, but three and thirtie sailes.

The fleete of *Terra Firma*, were at their first departure from *Spain*, 50. sailes, which were bound for *Nombre de Dios*, where they did discharge their lading, and thence returned to *Cartagena*, for their healths sake, untill the time the treasure was readie they should take in, at the said *Nombre de Dios*. But before this fleet departed, some

were gone by one or two at a time, so that only 23. sailes
of this fleete arrived in the *Havana*.

At the Hava-na there met	33. sailes of *Nova Hispania*.
	23. sailes of *Terra Firma*.
	12. sailes of *San Domingo*.
	9. sailes of *Hunduras*.

In the whole 77. ships, which joyned and set sailes
togither, at the *Havana*, the 17. of July, according to
our account, and kept togither untill they came into
the height of 35. degrees, which was about the tenth
of August, where they found the winde at Southwest,
chaunged sodenly to the North, so that the sea comming
out of the Southwest, and the winde very violent at North,
they were put all into great extremity, and then first
lost the Generall of their fleet, with 500. men in her ;
and within three or foure daies after an other storme
rising, there were five or six other of the biggest ships
cast away with all their men, togither with their vice
Admirall.

And in the height of 48. degrees about the end of
August, grew an other great storme, in which all the
fleet saving 48. sailes were cast away : which 48. sailes
kept togither, untill they came in sight of the Ilands
of *Corvo* and *Flores*, about the 5. or 6. of September, at
which time a great storme seperated them ; of which
number 15. or 16. were after seene by these Spanyards
to ride at anchor under the *Terçera* ; and twelve or
foureteene more to beare with the Iland of S. *Michaels* ;
what became of them after that these Spaniards were

taken, cannot yet be certified; their opinion is, that verie few of the fleet are escaped, but are either drowned or taken. And it is otherwaies of late certified, that of this whole fleet that should have come into *Spaine* this yeare, being 123. saile, there are as yet arrived but 25. This note was taken out of the examination of certaine Spaniards, that were brought into England by six of the ships of London, which tooke seven of the above named Indian fleet, neere the Ilands of *Açores*.

FINIS.

LONDON
Printed for William Ponsonbie.
1591.

LETTERS

I. A Relation of Cadiz Action in the year 1596. *written by Sir Walter Raleigh. Transcrib'd from a MS. in the Hands of his Grandchild, M*^r *Raleigh.*

YOu shall receive many relations, but none more true than this. May it please your honour therefore to know, that on Sunday being the 20th. of June the English fleet came to Anchor in the Bay of St. Sebastians,
10 short of Cales half a League. My Lord Admiral, being carefull of her Majesties Shipps, had resolved with the Earl of Essex, that the Town should be first attempted ; to the end, that both the Spanish Gallions, and Gallies, togeather with the forts of Cales might not all at once beat upon our navy. My self was not present at the resolution ; for I was sent the day before towards the mayn to stop such, as might pass out from S^t. Lucar, or Cales along the Coast. When I was arrived back again, (which was two houres after the rest) I found the Earl of
20 Essex disembarqueing his soldiers ; and he had put many companies into Boats purposeing to make his descent on the West side of Cales. But such was the greatness of the billow by reason of a forcible Southerly wind, as the boats were ready to sink at the stern of the Earl ; and

indeed divers did soe, and in them some of the armed men; but because it was formerly resolved (and that to cast doubts would have been esteemed an effect of feare) the Earl purposed to goe on, untill such time as I came aboard him, and in the presence of all the Colonells protested against the resolution; giving him reasons, and makeing apparent demonstrations, that he thereby ran the way of our generall ruin, to the utter overthrow of the whole armys, their own lives, and her Majesties future safety. The Earl excused himself, and layd it to the Lord Admirall, 10 who (he said) would not consent to enter with the fleet, till the Town were first possessed. All the Commanders, and Gentlemen present besought me to disswade the attempt; for they all perceived the danger, and were resolved, that the most part could not but perish in the Sea, ere they came to set foot on ground; and if any arrived on shoar, yet were they sure to have their boats cast on their heads, and that twenty in so desperate a descent would have defeated them all. The Earl hereupon prayed me to persuade my Lord Admirall; 20 who finding a certain destruction by the former resolution, was content to enter the Port. When I brought news of this agreement to the Earl, calling out of my boat upon him, Entramos; he cast his hat into the Sea for joy, and prepared to weigh anchor.

The day was now farr spent, and it required much time to return the boats of Soldiers to their own shipps; so as we could not that night attempt the fleet, although many (seeming desperatly valiant) thought it a fault of mine to put it off till the morning; albeit we had neither 30 agreed in what manner to fight, nor appointed, who should lead, and who should second, whether by boarding, or otherwise ; neither could our fleet possibly recover all their men in before Sun-sett : But both the generalls being pleased to hear me, and many times to be advised by so mean an understanding, came again to an anchor in the very mouth of the harbour : So that night about ten of the clock I wrote a Letter to the Lord Admirall, declaring therin my opinion, how the fight should be ordered ; persuading him to appoint to each of the great Gallions of Spain two great fly boats to board them, after such time as the Queens shipps had battered them ; for I knew, that both the S^t. Philip, and the rest would burn, and not yeild ; and then to loose so many of the Queens for company I thought it too dear a purchase, and it would be termed but a lamentable Victory.

This being agreed on, and both the Generalls per- suaded to lead the body of the fleet, the charge for the performance thereof was (upon my humble suit) granted, and assigned unto me. The Shipps appointed to second me were these :

The Mary Rose, commanded by Sir George Carew ; The Lyon, by Sir Robert Southwell ; The Rainbow, by the Marshall, Sir Fr. Veare ; The Swiftsure, by Captain Cross ; The Dreadnaught, by Sir Conyers, and Alex. Clifford ; The Nonparill, by M^r. Dudley ; The 12. shipps of London with certain flyboats.

The Lord Tho. Howard, because the Meere-honour, which he commanded, was one of the greatest shipps, was also left behind with the Generalls ; but being impatient therof pressed the Generalls to have the service committed unto him, and left the Meer-honour to Mr. Dudley, putting himself into the Nonparilla. For mine own part, as I was willing to give honour to my Lord Thomas, having both precedency in the Army, and being a Nobleman, whom I much honourd ; so yet I was resolved to give, and not take Example for this service, holding mine own reputation dearest, and remembring my great duty to her Majestie. With the first peep of 10 day therefore I weighed anchor, and bare with the Spanish fleet, taking the start of all ours a good distance.

Now Sir, may it please you to understand, that there were ranged under the wall of Cales, on which the Sea beateth, Seaventeen Gallies, which lay with their prowes to flank our entrance, as we passed towards the Gallions. There was also a fort called the Philip, which beat, and commanded the harbour. There were also ordnance, which lay all alongst the Curtain upon the Wall towards the Sea : there were also divers other peeces of Culverin, 20 which also scoured the channell. Notwithstanding, as soon as the S^t. Philip perceived one of the Admiralls under saile approaching, she also set saile, and with her the S^t. Matthew, the S^t. Thomas, the S^t. Andrew, the two great Gallions of Lysbon, three frigotts of warr accustomed to transport the treasure, two Argosies very strong in Artillery, the Admirall, Vice Admirall, and Rear Admirall of Nueva Espagna, with forty other great shipps bound for Mexico, and other places : Of all which the S^t. Philip, the S^t. Mathew, the S^t. Andrew, 30

and the S^t. Thomas, being fowr of the Royall Shipps of Spain, came again to anchor under the fort of Puntall, in a streight of the harbour, which leadeth towards Puerto Reall : On the right hand of them they placed the three frigotts ; on the back the two Gallions of Lysbon, and the Argosies ; and the 17. Gallies by three, and three to interlace them, as occasion should be offered. The Admirall, Vice-Admirall, and Rear-Admirall of Nueva Espagna, with the body of the fleet, were placed
10 behind them towards Puerto Reall ; hoping with this great strength to defend the entrance, the place being no broader from point to point than that these did in effect stretch over as a bridge, and had besides the fort of Puntall to their guard. But the 17. Gallies did not at the first depart with the rest, but stayed by the Town with all their Prowes bent against us, as we entred ; with which togeather with the Artillery of the Town, and forts they hoped to have stumbled the leading shipp, and doubted not thereby but to have discouraged the rest.
20 Haveing, as aforesaid, taken the leading, I was first saluted by the fort called Philip, afterward by the ordnance on the Curtain, and lastly by all the Gallies in good order. To show scorn to all which, I only answered first the fort, and afterward the Gallies, to each peece a Blurr with a trumpet ; disdaining to shoot one peece at any one, or all of those esteemed-dreadfull monsters. The shipps, that followed, beat upon the Gallies so thick as they soon betook them to their Oars, and gott up to joyne with the Gallions in the streight, as aforesaid ; and
30 then as they were driven to come near me, and inforced

to range their sides towards me, I bestowed a benediction amongst them.

But S[t]. Philip, the great, and famous Admirall of Spain was the mark I shott at; esteeming those Gallies but as wasps, in respect of the powerfullness of the other; and being resolved to be revenged for the Revenge, or to second her with mine own life, I came to anchor by the Gallions; of which the Philip, and Andrew were two, that boarded the Revenge. I was formerly commanded not to board, but was promised fly-boats, in which after I had 10 battered a while I resolved to joyn unto them.

My Lord Thomas came to anchor by me on the one hand with the Lyon; the Mary Rose on the other with the Dreadnaught; the Marshall toward the side of Puntall; and towards ten of the clock my Lord Generall Essex, being impatient to abide farr off, hearing so great thunder of Ordnance, thrust up through the fleet, and headed all those on the left hand, comeing to anchor next unto me on that side; and afterward came in the Swiftsure, as neare as she could. Allwaies I must without 20 glory say for my self, that I held single in the head of all.

Now after we had beat, as two Butts, one upon another almost 3 hours, (assuring your honour, that the Vollyes of Canon, and Culverin came as thick, as if it had been a skirmish of Musketteers) and finding my self in danger to be sunk in the place, I went to my Lord Generall in my Skiff to desire him, that he would inforce the promised fly-boats to come up, that I might board; for as I ridd, I could not endure so great a battery any long time: my Lord Generall was then coming up himself; to whom 30

I declared, that if the fly-boats came not, I would board
with the Queen's shipp ; for it was the same loss to burn,
or sink ; for I must endure the one. The Earl finding,
that it was not in his power to command fear, told me,
that whatsoever I did, he would second me in person upon
his honour. My Lord Admirall haveing also a disposition to come up at first, but the River was so choaked,
as he could not pass with the Ark, came up in person into
the Nonperilla, with my Lord Thomas.

10   While I was thus speaking with the Earl, the Marshal
who thought it some touch to his great esteemed Valour
to ride behind me so many houres, gott up a head my
shipp ; which my Lord Thomas perceiving headed him
again, my self being but a quarter of an hour absent.
At my return finding my self from being the first, to be
but the third ; I presently let slipp Anchor, and thrust in
between my Lord Thomas, and the Marshall, and went
up farther a head than all them before, and thrust my
self a thwart the Channell, so as I was sure, none should
20 outstart me again for that day. My Lord Generall
Essex thinking his shipps sides stronger than the rest,
thrust the Dreadnaught aside, and came next the Warr-
spight on the left hand a head all that Rank, but my
Lord Thomas. The Marshall, while we had not leisure
to look behind us, secretly fastened a rope on my shipps
side towards him, to draw himself up equally with me ;
but some of my company advertiseing me therof, I caused
it to be cut off, and so he fell back into his place ; whom
I guarded all but his very prow from the sight of the
30 Enemy.

Now if it please you to remember, that having no hope of my fly-boats to bord, and that the Earl, and my Lord Thomas both promised to second me; I layd out a warp by the side of the Philip to shake hands with her (for with the wind we could not get aboard :) Which when she, and the rest perceived, finding also that the Repulse (seeing mine) began to doe the like, and the Rear-Admirall my Lord Thomas; they all let slipp, and rann a ground, tumbling into the sea heaps of Soldiers, so thick, as if coals had been poured out of a sack, in many 10 Ports at once, some drowned, and some sticking in the Mudd. The Philip, and the S^t. Thomas burnt themselves; the S^t. Matthew, and the S^t. Andrew were recovered by our boats, ere they could get out to fire them. The spectacle was very lamentable on their side; for many drowned themselves; many half burnt leapt into the water; very many hanging by the ropes ends by the Shipps side under the water even to the lipps; many swimming with grieveous wounds, strucken under water, and put out of their pain; and withall so huge a fire, and 20 such tearing of the Ordnance in the great Philip, and the rest, when the fire came to them, as if any man had a desire to see Hell it self, it was there most lively figured. Our Selves spared the lives of all after the Victory; but the Flemmings, who did little, or nothing in the fight, used merciless slaughter, till they were by my self, and afterward by my Lord Admirall beaten off.

The shipps, that abode the fight in the morning till tenn a clock, were the Wast-Spight, the Nonparilla, the Lyon, the Mary Rose, the Rainbow, and the Dreadnaught. 30

To second these came up the Earl, and the Swiftsure : and these were all that did ought against six goodly Gallions, two Argosies, three Frigotts, Seaventeen Gallies, and the fort of Puntall, backd by the Admirall of Nueva Espagna, and others ; in all, 55, or 57.

This being happily finished, we prepared to land the Army, and to attempt the Town ; in which there were of all sorts some 5000. foot Burgers, 150. soldiers in pay, and some 800. horse of the Gentry, and Cavalleros of Xerez, gathered togeather upon the discovery of our fleet two daies before, while we were becalmed off Cape S^t. Mary. The horsmen sallyed out to resist the Landing ; but were so well withstood, that they most took their way toward the Bridge, which leadeth into the Mayn, called Puento Souse ; the rest retired to the Town, and so hardly followed, as they were driven to leave their horses at the Port, (which the Inhabitants durst not open to let them in) and so they leapt down an old Wall into the Suburbs ; and being so closely followed by the Vauntguard of our footmen, as when the Generall perceived an Entrance there, he thought it was possible for ours to do the like ; upon which occasion the Town was carryed with a sudden fury, and with little loss ; onely Sir John Wingfeild was slayn, Sir Edward Wingfeild, Captain Bagnall, and Captain Medick hurt ; other men of quality few, or none.

For the particular behaviours of any, that entred, I cannot otherwise deliver, than by report ; for I received a greivous blow in my legg, interlaced, and deformed with splinters in the fight ; yet being desirous to see every man's disposition, I was carryed ashoare on mens shoulders; and as soon as my horse was recovered, my Lord Admirall sent one unto me, but I was not able to abide above an houre in the Town for the torment I suffered, and for the fear I had to be shouldred in the press, and among the tumultuous disordered soldiers; that being then given to spoyl, and rapin had no respect. The same night I returned, chiefly for that there was no Admirall left to order the fleet, and (indeed) few, or no people in the navy; all running headlong to the Sack: 10 and secondly because I was unfit for ought but ease at that time.

At the break of day following I sent to the Generalls to have order to follow the fleet of Shipps bound for the Indies; which were said to be worth twelve millions, and lay in Puerte Reall-Rode, where they could not escape: But the Town new taken, and the confusion great, it was allmost impossible for them to order many things at once; so as I could not receive any answer to my desire.

The afternoon of the same day those, which were 20 Merchants of Cales, and Sivill, offered the Generalls two millions to spare that fleet; whereupon there was nothing done for the present; But the morning following, being the 23d. of June, the Duke of Medina caused all that fleet of merchants to be set on fire; because he was resolved, that they must needs have fallen into our hands. So as now both Gallions, frigotts, Argosies, and all other shipps of warr, togeather with the fleet of Nueva Espagna, were all converted into ashes; onely the S^t. Matthew, and the S^t. Andrew were in our possession. 30

Much of the Ordnance of the S^t. Philip hath been saved
by the Flemmings, who have had great Spoile.   There is
imbarked good store of Ordnance out of the Town ; and
the 2. Apostles aforesaid are well furnished, which (God
willing) we purpose to bring into England.   The Town
of Cales was very rich in merchandise, in plate, and
money ;   many rich Prisoners given to the land Commanders, so as that sort are very rich.   Some had Prisoners
for 16000 Ducatts ; some for 20000 ; some for 10000 ;
10 and besides, great houses of Merchandise.   What the
Generalls have gotten, I know least ;   they protest it
is little : for mine own part I have gotten a lame legg,
and a deformed ; for the rest, either I spake too late,
or it was otherwise resolved.   I have not wanted good
words, and exceeding kind, and regardfull usage ; but
I have possession of naught, but poverty, and pain.   If
God had spared me that blow, I had possessd my self of
some house.

II. Sir Walter Rawleigh to his wife after he
20 *had hyrte himselfe in the tower* [1603].

REceyve from thy unfortunate husband theis his last
lynes, theis the last words that ever thou shalt receive
from him.   That I can live to thinke never to see the, and
my child more, I cannot, I have desired god and disputed
with my reason, but nature and Compassion hath the
victorie.   That I can live to thinke howe you are both

lefte a spoile to my enimies, and that my name shalbe
a dishonour to my child, I cannot, I cannot indure the
memorie thereof.   Unfortunate woman, unfortunate
Child, comfort your selves, trust god, and be contented
with your poore estate, I woulde have bettered it, if
I had enjoyed a fewe yeares.   Thowe art a yong woman
and forbeare not to marry againe, it is nowe nothing
to me, thowe art noe more mine, nor I thine. To witnes
that thowe didest love me once, take care that thowe
marry not to please sence, but to avoide povertie and to 10
preserve thy child. That thowe didest also love me livinge,
witnesse it to others, to my poore daughter, to whome
I have geven nothinge, for his sake whoe wilbe cruell
to himselfe to preserve the.   Be Charitable to her, and
teach thy sonne to love her for his father's sake.   For
my selfe I am left of all men that have done good to many.
All my good turnes forgotten, all my errours revived, and
expounded to all extremitie of ill.   All my services,
hazardes, and expenses, for my Countrie plantings,
discoveries, fights, Councells, and whatsoever ells, malice 20
hath nowe covered over, I am nowe made an enimie
and traytour by the word of an unworthie man, he hath
proclaimed me to be a partaker of his vaine imaginacions,
notwithstanding the whole Course of my life hath
approved the contrarie, as my death shall approve it.
Woe, woe, woe, be unto him by whose falsehood we are
loste, he hath seperated us asunder, he hath slaine my
honour, my fortune, he hath robbed the of thy husband,
thy child of his father, and me of you both.   Oh god
thowe doest knowe my wronges, knowe then thowe my 30

wife and child, knowe then thowe my Lord and kinge
that I ever thought them to honest to betraie, and too
good to conspire againste. But my wife forgeve thowe
all, as I doe, live humble, for thowe hast but a time also,
God forgeve my Lord Harry, for he was my heavie
enimye, And for my Lord Cecill I thought he woulde
never forsake me in extremitie, I woulde not have done
it him, god knowes, But doe not thowe knowe it, for
he muste be maister of thy Child, and maye have com-
10 passion of him. Be not dismaide that I dyed in dispaire
of gods mercies, strive not to dispute it but assure thy
selfe that god hath not lefte me nor Sathan tempted me.
Hope and dispaire live not together, I knowe it is forbidden to destroye our selves but I trust it is forbidden
in this sorte, that we destroye not our selves dispairinge
of gods mercie.

The mercie of god is immesurable, the cogitacions of
men comprehend it not, In the lord I have ever trusted,
and I knowe that my redeemer lyveth, farr is it from me
20 to be tempted with Sathan, I am onely tempted with
sorrowe, whose sharpe teeth devoure my harte. O god
that art goodnes it selfe, thowe canst not be but good to
me, oh god that art mercye it selfe, thowe canst not be
but mercifull to me. For my State [it] is conveyed to
Feoffees, to your Cosen Brett and others, I have but
a bare estate for a shorte life. My plate is at gage in
Lumberd streete, my debts are many. To Peter Vanlore
some 600^{li}, To Antrobus as much, but Cumpton is to paye
300^{li} of it. To michaell Hext 100^{ll}, To George Carewe
30 100^{li}, To Nicholas Sanders 100^{li}, to John Fitz James

100^{li}, To Master Waddonn 100^{li}, To a poore man one
Hawker for horses 70^{li}, To a poore man called Hance
20^{li}, take first care of those for gods sake. To a brewer
at Weymouth, and a Baker for my Lord Cecills Shippe
and myne, I thinke some 80^{li}, John Renolds knoweth it.
And let that poore man have his true part of my Retorne
from Virginia, and let the poore mens wages be paid
with the goods, for the lords sake, Oh what will my poore
servannts thinke at their retourne, when they heare I am
accused to be Spanish, whoe sente them to my greate 10
Charge to plant and discover upon his territorie, Oh
intollerable infamie, Oh god I cannot resiste theis thoughts,
I cannot live to thinke howe I am deryded, to thinke of
the expectacion of my enimyes, the scornes I shall receive,
the crewell words of lawyers, the infamous tauntes and
dispightes, to be made a wonder and a spectacle. O death
hasten the unto me, that thowe maiste destroye the
memorie of theis, and laye me up in darke forgetfullnes.
O death destroye my memorie which is my Tormentour,
my thoughts and my life cannot dwell in one body. But 20
doe thowe forget me poore wife, that thowe maist
live to bring up thy poore Child, I recommend unto you
my poore brother A. Gilbert. The lease of Sandring
is his and none of myne, lett him have it for gods cause,
he knowes what is due to me upon it, and be good to
Kemis, for he is a perfecte honest man, and hath much
wronge for my sake. For the rest I commend me to
them, and them to god. And the Lord knowes my sorrowe
to part from the and my poore Child, but part I must
by enimyes and Injuries, parte with shame, and triumph 30

of my detractours, And therefore be contented with this
worke of god, and forget me in all things but thine owne
honour, and the love of mine. I blesse my poore child,
And let him knowe his father was noe traytour. Be bold
of my Innocencie, for god to whome I offer life and soule
knowes it. And whosoever thowe chuse againe after
me, lett him be but thy politique husband, but let my
sonne be thy beloved, for he is parte of me, and I live
in him, and the difference is but in the nomber, and not
10 in the kinde, And the Lord for ever keepe the and them,
and geve the comfort in both worlds.

III. *The Coppy of a Letter, written by Sir Walter Raleigh, to his wife, the Night before hee expected to be putt to death att winchester.* 1603.

YOu shall nowe receive (my deare wife) my last words,
in these my last lynes, my Love I send you, that
you may keepe itt, when I am dead, and my Counsell
that you may remember itt, when I am noe more;
20 I would not by my will present you with Sorrowes (Deare
Besse). Lett them goe into the grave with mee; and
bee buried in the dust, And seeing itt is not the will of
God, that I shall see you any more in this life, beare itt
patiently, and with an heart like thy selfe.

First I send you all the thankes, which my heart Can
Conceive, or my words can expresse for your many travailes,

and Care taken for mee, which though they have not taken effect, as you wished, yett my debt to you, is not the lesse, but pay itt I never shall, in this world.

Secondly I beseech you, for the love you bare mee liveing, doe not hide your selfe many dayes, after my death, but by your Travailes seeke to help your miserable fortunes, and the Right of your poore Child, Thy mournings Cannot availe mee, I am but dust.

Thirdly you shall understand, that my Land was Conveyed Bona fide to my Childe, The writeings weere 10 drawne att Midsommer twelve monthes, my honest Cosen Brett, can testifie soe much, and Dalberrie too, Cann remember somewhat therein, And I trust my blood, will quench the[ir] Malice, that have thus Cruelly murthered mee, And that they will not seeke alsoe to kill thee and thine with extreame povertie.

To what freind to direct thee, I knowe not, for all mine have left mee, in the true tyme of triall; And I plainely perceive, that my death was determyned from the first day. 20

Most sorrie I am (God knowes) that being thus surprised with death, I can Leave you in noe better estate, God is my wittnesse, I meant you all my office of wynes, or all that I could have purchased by sellinge itt, halfe my stuffe, and all my Jewells, But some on't for the Boy, but god hath prevented all my Resolutions, and even that great god that ruleth all in all; But if you Can live free from want, Care for noe more; the rest is but vanitie.

Love God, and beginn betymes, to repose your selfe 30

on him, and therein shall you finde true and lasting
Riches, and endlesse Comfort, For the rest when you
have travailled and wearied all your thoughts, over all
sorts of worldly Cogitations, you shall but sitt downe by
sorrowe in the end.

Teach your sonne alsoe to love and feare god whilst
hee is yett younge, that the feare of god may growe upp
with him ; and the same God will bee a husband to you,
and a Father to him, A husband, and a Father, which
10 Cannot bee taken from you.

Baylie oweth mee 200^{li} and Adrian Gilbert 600^{li}.
In Jersey, I have alsoe much monye oweing mee, Besides
the Arrerages of the Wynes will pay my debts. And
howsoever you doe, for my soules sake, pay all poore men.

When I am gone, noe doubt you shall bee sought by
many ; for the world thinks, that I was very rich. But
take heed of the pretences of men, and theire affections ;
For they last not but in honest, and worthie Men ; And
noe greater misery can befall you in this life, then to
20 become a prey, and afterwards to bee dispised : I speake
not this (god knowes) to disswade you from marriage, for
itt will bee best for you, both in respect of the world
and of God.

As for mee, I am noe more yours, nor you mine, Death
hath Cutt us a sunder ; and God hath devided mee from
the world, and you from mee.

Remember your poore Child, for his Fathers sake,
who chose you, and Loved you, in his happiest tymes.

Gett those Letters (if it bee possible) which I writt to
30 the Lords, wherein I sued for my life, God is my wittnesse,

Itt was for you and yours I desired life. Butt itt is true that I disdaine my selfe for begging itt, For knowe it (deare wife) that your sonne, is the sonne of a true man, and one, whoe in his owne respect, dispiseth Death, and all his mishapen and ouglye shapes.

I cannot write much : God hee knowes, howe hardly, I steale this tyme, while others sleepe ; and itt is alsoe high tyme, that I should seperate my thoughts from the world.

Begg my dead body, which Liveinge was denyed thee ; 10 and either Laye itt att Shirbourne (if the Land Continue) or in Excester Church by my Father and Mother.

I can say noe more, tyme and death call me away.

The everlasting, powerfull, infinite and omnipotent god, that Almightie God, whoe is goodnesse itt selfe, the true life, and true light, keepe thee, and thine ; have mercye on mee, and teach mee to forgive my persecutors and Accusers, and send us to meete in his glorious kingdome.

My deare wife farewell, Blesse my poore Boye, Pray 20 for mee, and Lett my Good god hold you both in his armes.

Written with the dyeing hand of sometyme thy Husband, but now (alasse) overthrowne   Wa : Raleigh.

      yours that was, But nowe not
      my owne.
       W : R :

*IV. Copie of Sir Walter Raleigh's Letter [to
Sir Ralph Winwood] of 21° Martii, 1617
[Old Style].*

SIr, As I have not hitherto given you any account of
our proceedings, and passage towards the Indyes, so
have I no other subject to write of since our aryvalle,
then of the greatest and sharpest misfortunes, that
have ever befallen any man. For whereas for the first
all those that navigate betweene Capo Verde and America,
10 doe passe it in *15* or *20* dayes at most, we found the
winds so contrary (which is also contrary to nature) and
so many violent stormes, and raynes, as wee spent six
weeks in that passage, by reason whereof and that in so
great heate, we wanted water (for at the Ile Bravo of
cap de Verd, we lost our cables and anchors, and our
water cask, being driven from the Island with a hurlican,
and weare all lyke to have perished) great sicknes fell
amongst us and caryed away great numbers of our
hablest men boath for sea and land.   The 17.
20 of November we had sight of the coast of Guiana, and
soone after came to anchor in fyve degrees at the river
Caliana. heere we stayed, till the 4th of december,
landed our sick men, sett up the barges and shallups,
which we brought out of England in quarters, washt
our ships and tooke in fresh water, being fedd and assisted
by the Indyans of my ould acquaintance, with a greate
deale of love and respect. My selfe haveing beene in
the hands of death without hope som *6* weeks (and not

yet hable otherwise to moove, then as I was caryed in
a chayre) gave order to fyve small shipps to sayle into
Orenoke, haveing Captain Kemish, for theyre conductor
towardes the myne, and in those five shipps fyve companyes
of fifty under the command [of Captain] Parker and
Captain North, brothers to the Lord mounteagle and
the Lord north, valient gentlemen, and of [infinite]
patience, for the labor, hunger, and heate which they
have [endured] ; my sonne had the third company,
captain Thornix of kent [the f]ourth : Captain Chudlay, 10
(by his lieutenant) the fifth. But as [my] sargent major
Captain Pigott of the low contryes dyed in [the] former
miserable passage ; so my lieutenant Sir warham [Saint
Le]ger lay sick without hope of lyfe, and the charge
conferrd [on] my nephew George Raleigh, who had also
served long, with singular [com]mendacions, in the low
contryes, but (by reason of my absence, and of Sir
Warrhams), was not so well obeyed, as the enterprise
required. As they past up the river, the Spaniards
began the warre and sho[t] at us, both with their ordenance 20
and Muskets : whereuppon the Companies were forst
to charge them, and soone after beate them out of their
towne. In the assault whereof my Sonne, having more
desire of honor, then of safety, was slayne, and with
whome (to say the truth) all respect of the world hath
taken end in me. And although these five Captaines
had as weake Companies as ever followed valiant leaders ;
yet were there amongst them som[e 2]o or 30 [ve]ry adventurous gentlemen, and of singular courage [as of my
sonne's] Companie, Mr. Knevet, Mr. Hamon, Mr. 30

Langw[orth, Mr. John] Plesington, his officers; Sir
John Hamden, [Mr. Simon Leak] (Corporall of the field)
Mr. Hammens elder brother; [Mr. Nicholas] of Bucking-
ham, Mr. Roberts of Kent, Mr. Perin, Mr. Tr[esham],
Mr. Mullinax, Mr. Winter, and his brother, Mr. Way,
Mr. Miles Herbert, Mr. William Herbert, Mr. Bradshaw,
Captain Hall and others. Sir, I set downe the names
of these Gentlemen, to the end that if his Majestie shall
have cause to use their service, it may please you to
10 take knowledge of them for very sufficient men. The
other five ships stayed at Trinidado, having no other Port
capable of them neere Guiana. The second
ship was commaunded by my Viceadmirall Captain John
Penington, of whome (to doe him right) I must confesse,
that he is one of the sufficientest gentlemen for the Sea,
that England hath. The third, by Sir Warrham S^t
Leger, an exceeding valiant, and worthy Gentleman.
The fourth, by Sir John Ferne, and the fift, by Captain
Chydley of Devon. With these five ships I dayly attended
20 the Armada of Spaine, which had they set uppon us, our
force divided, (the one half in Orenoque, a hundred and
fiftie miles from us) wee had not onely bene torne in peeces,
but all those in the river had also perished, being of no
defence at all for a sea fight. For wee had resolved
to have burnt by their sides, and to have dyed there,
had the Armada arrived. But belike they stay for us
at Marguerita, by which they know wee must pas[se
towards the] Indies.

For it pleased his Majestie to value us at [so little, as
30 to com]maund me, uppon my allegeance, to sett downe

[under my hand the] countrey, and the very river by which I was to ente[r it, to set down] the number of my men, and burden of my ships, with [what ordnance] every ship caryed; which being made knowne to the [Spanish ambas]sador, and by him in post to the King of Spaine, a d[espatch was] made by him, and his letters sent from Madril, before my departure out of the Thames. For his first letter sent by a Barke of Advise, was dated the 19th of March, 1617, at Madril; which letter I have here-inclosed sent your Honour: the rest 10 I reserve not knowing whether these may be intercepted or not. The second of the Kings dated the 17th of May, sent also by a Caravell to Diego de Palomeque, Governor of Guiana, El Dorado, and Trinidado: the third by the Bishop of Puerto-ricco, and delivered to Palomeque the 15th of July at Trinidado: and the 4th was sent from the farmer and Secretarie of his Customes in the Indies at the same time. By that of the Kings hand [brought] by the Bishop there was also a Commission for the speedy levying of 300 [soldie]rs, and ten peeces of ordenance, 20 to be sent from Puerto-ricco for the de[fence of] Guiana, a hundred and 50 from Nuevo Reino de Granado under the Com[mand] of Captain Antonio Musica, and the other 150 from Puerto-rico to be [condu]cted by Captain Francisco Zanchio. Now Sir, if all that have traded the Indies since his Majesties time know it, that the Spaniards have flayed alive these poore men which they have taken, being but Marchant men, what death and torment shall wee expect, if they conquer us? Certainely they have hitherto fayled grossely, being set out unto them as wee 30

were, both for our numbers, time, and place. Lastly
to make an Apologie for not working the Mine, although
I know not (his Majestie excepted) whome I am to
satisfie so much as my self, having lost my sonne,
and my estate in the enterprise ; yet it is true, that the
Spaniards tooke more care to defend the passages leading
unto it, then they did their towne, which (say the
Kings instructions) they might easily doe, the country
being aspera et fragosa ; but it is true, that when Kemish
10 founde the rivers low, and that he could not approach
the bankes in most places neere the Mine by a mile,
and where he founde a descent, a volley of Muskets came
from the woodes uppon the Bankes, and slew two of
the rowers, hurt six others, and shot a valiant Gentleman
Captain Thornix in the heade, of which wounde he hath
languished to this day : He (to wit, Kemish) following
his owne advise, that it was in vaine to discover the Mine
(for he gave me this for excuse, at his returne, that the
Companies of English in their towne of St. Thome were
20 hardly able to defend it against the dayly and nightly
alarmes and assaults of the Spaniards, that the passage
to the mine was of thicke and impassable woodes ; that
being discovered, they had no men to worke it) did not
discover it at all. For it is true, that the Spaniards, having
two gold mines neere the towne, the one possessed by
Petro Rodrigo de Parama, the second [mine by He]rnian
Fruntino, the third of silver by Francisco Fashardo, [left
them] for the want of Negros to worke them. For as
the Indians cannot [be constrai]ned, by a Law of Charles
30 the fift, so the Spaniard will not, [neither can] they endure

the labor of these Mines, whatsoever that Brag[gadochi]o the Spanish Embassador say, I shall prove it under the Proprietaries [hand, by] the Custome bookes, and by the Kings Quinto of which I recovered an [ingot] or two, and I shall make it appeare to any Prince or state, that [will] undertake it, how easily these Mines and five or six more may be [possess]t, and the most of them in those places, which never yet have bene attempted by any enemie, nor any passage unto them ever discovered by the English, Dutch, or French. But at Kemishes returne from Orenoque, when I rejected his Counsell and his course, and told him, that he had undone me, and wounded my credite with the King past recoverie, he slew himself. For I told him, that seing my sonne w[as] lost, I cared not, if he had lost a hundred more in opening the Min[e,] so my credite had bene saved. For I protest before god, had not Ca[ptain] Whitney, (whome I gave more countenance unto, then to [a]ll the Capt[aines] of my fleete) runne from me at the Granados, and car[ried] another ship with him of Captain Wollastons, I would have left [my bodie] at St. Thome by my sonnes, or have brought with me out [of that or] other Mines so much gold ore, as should have satisfied [the King that] I had propounded no vaine thing.

What shall become of me now, I know not ; I am unpardo[ned] in England, and my poore estate consumed, and whether any other Prince or State will give me breade, I know not. I desire your Honour to hold me in your good opinion, and to remember my service to my Lords of Arundell, and Pembroke : to take some 30

pitie on my poore wife, to whome I dare not write for
renewing the sorrow for her sonne : and beseech you,
to give a Copie of these to my Lord Carew : for to a
broken minde, to a weake bodie, and weake eyes it is
a torment to write many letters. I have founde many
thinges of importance for discovering the estate and
weakenes of the Indies, which if I live, I shall hereafter
impart unto your Honor, to whome I shall ever remaine
a faithfull servant,   W. RALEGH.

10   Sir, since the death of Kemish, it is confest by the
Sergeant-Major and other of his inward friendes, that
he told them, when they were at the Rivers mouth coming
thence, that he could have brought them to the Mine
within two howers march from the rivers side, but
because my sonne was slayne, my self unpardoned, and not
like to live, he had no reason to open the Mine either for
the Spaniards, or for the King. They aunswered, that
the King ([though] I were not pardoned) had graunted
me my pa[tent under the great] Seale : he replyed, that
20 the graunt to me was [to a man who] was non ens in law,
and therefore of no fo[rce. This discourse] he had,
which I knew not of, till after h[is death :] when I was
resolved to write to your Hon[our, he prayed] me ;
to joyne with him in excusing his not go[ing to the]
Mine ; I aunswered him that I would not doe [it ; that] if
himself could satisfie the King and the State, that he had
reason not to open it, I should be glad of it ; but for my
part I must avow it, that he knew it, and that he might
with litle losse have done it : other excuse I would not

frame. He then told me, that he would waite on me presently and give me better satisfaction : but I was no sooner come from him into my Cabin, but I heard a pistoll goe of over my heade, and sending up, to know who shott it, word was brought, that Kemish had shott it out of his Cabin window to clense it ; his boy going into the Cabin founde him lying on his bed with much bloude by him, and looking on his face, saw he was deade : the Pistoll being but litle, the bullet did but cracke his ribb ; but he turning him over, founde a long knife in 10 his bodie, all but the handle.

Sir, I have sent into England in a flyboate, with my coosen Herbert (a very valiant, and honest gentleman) diverse other unworthy persons, good for nothing either by land or sea, and though it was at their owne suite, yet I know, that they will wrong me in all they can. I beseech your Honour that this scumme of men may not be beleeved of me, who have taken more paine, and suffered more, then the meanest rascall in the ship. These being gone, I shalbe able, if I live, to keepe the 20 sea till the end of August with fower reasonable good ships.

Sir whensoever god shall permitt me to arrive in any part of Europe, I will not faile to let your Honour know what wee have done. Till then and ever

Your Honours servant
WRALEGH.

From St. Christophers one
of the Ilandes of the Antillias,
the 21th of March *1617*.   30

V. The Coppie of a Letter written by Sir Walter Raleigh, to his wife, from the Isle of St. Christophers, touching the ill successe of his last voyage to Guiana, bearing date the 22th of March, 1617. [Old Style]

I Was loath to write, because I know not, howe to comfort you, And God knowes, I never knewe what sorrow meant till now.   All that I can say to you, is, that you
10 must obey the will and providence of god, and remember, that the Queenes Majestie bare the losse of Prince Henry, with a magnanimous heart, and the Lady Harrington of her onely sonne.   Comfort your heart (Deare Besse) I shall sorrow for us both : and I shall sorrowe the lesse, because I have not longe to sorrowe, because I have not longe to live. I referr you to Mr. Secretaryes Wynwoods Letter ; whoe will give you a Coppy of it, if you send for itt, Therein you shall knowe what hath past, what I have written by that Letter, For my braines are
20 broken, and tis a torment to mee, to write, espetially of miserye : I have desired Mr. Secretary, to give my Lord Carew, a Coppie of his Letter. I have clensed my shipp of sicke men, and sent them home ; and hope, that god will send us somewhat, ere wee returne.   Comend mee to all att Loathbury.   You shall heare from

mee, if I live, from newe found Land, where I meane to
Cleane my shipp and revictuall ; For I have Tobacco
enough, to pay for itt.   The Lord blesse you, and Comfort
you, that you may beare patiently, the death of your most
valiant sonne.

Your Wal: Raleigh:

March the 22th from the
Isle of St. Christophers.

Postscript.

I protest before the Majestie of God, that as Sir
Francis Drake, and Sir John Hawkins died heart broken,
when they failed of their enterprise, I would willingly
doe the like, did I not Contend with sorrowe, to Comfort,
and releive you, if I Live to returne, resolve your selfe,
that itt is the Care for you, that hath strengthned my
heart.   Itt is true that Kemish, might have gone directly
to the myne, and meant itt, But after my sonnes death,
hee made them beleive, that hee knewe not the way, and
excused him self upon the want of water in the River,
and Counterfeiting many impedments, left itt unfound.
When hee came backe, I told him that hee had undone
mee, and that my Creditt was lost for ever, Hee aunswered
that when my sonne was lost, hee left mee soe weake, as
hee resolved, not to finde mee alive, hee had noe reason
to enrich a Company, whoe after my sonnes death,
made noe account of him ; Hee further told mee, that the
English, sent upp into Guyana, Could hardly defend the
Spanish Towne of St. Thome, which they had taken :
And therefor, for them, to passe through the thicke woods,

it was impossible, and more impossible, to have victuall
brought them into the mountaine. And it is true, that
the Governour Diego Polemeque, and fower other
Captaines beinge slaine (of which my sonne Watt slew
one) Plessington (Watts serjeaunt) and John of Maroccos,
(one of his men) slew each two) I say five of them slaine,
in the entrance of the Towne, the rest went of in a whole
body ; and tooke more Care to defend the passages to
their mynes (of which they had three, within a League
10 of the Towne, besides [a] myne, which was about five
myles of) then they did of the Cittie itt selfe : yet
Kemish att the first, was resolved to goe to the myne,
But when hee came to the bankes side to Lande, hee had
two of his men slaine out-right from the Banke, six
others hurt, and Captaine Thornex shott in the head,
of which wound, and the Accidents thereof, hee hath
pined awaye, this twelve weekes,   Now when
Kemish came backe and gave mee the former reasons,
which moved him not to open the Myne, The one the
20 death of my sonne, the second, the weakenesse of the
English, and their impossibillitye, to worke itt, and to bee
victualled, a third that itt was folly to discover itt for
the Spanyard ; and the last both my weaknesse, and my
being unpardoned : And that I rejected all these Arguments, and told him I must leave him to himself, to
aunswer itt to the Kinge and the state, hee shutt himselfe
into his Cabbin, and shott himselfe, with a pockett pistoll,
which brake one of his Ribbs, And findeing that itt had
not prevailed, hee thrust a longe knife under his short
30 Ribbs, upp to the handle, and dyed.   This

much I have writt to Mr. Secretary, to whose Letters, I referr you. But because I thinke my Freinds, will rather hearken after you, then any other, to knowe the truth, I did after the sealeing, breake open your Letter againe, to Lett you know in breife, the state of that businesse, which I pray impart to my Lord of Northumberland, and Sil Skory, and to Sir John Leigh.

For the rest, there was never poore man, soe exposed, to the slaughter, as I was, for beinge Commaunded upon my Allegiance, to sett downe, not onely the Country, but the very River by which I was to enter itt, to name my shipps, number my men, and my Artillery, This was sent by the Spanish Ambassadour, to his Master the kinge, The king wrote his Letters, to all parts of the Indyes, and espetially to the Governour Polomeque of Guiana, Eldorado, and Trinidado, of which, the first Letter bare date, the 19th of March, att Madrid, when I had not yett left the Thames, which Letter, I have sent Mr. Secretary. I have alsoe two other Letters of the kings, which I reserve, and one of the Counsell. The kinge alsoe sent a Commission to Levy 300 soldiers, out of his Garrison of Nuevo Reigno de Granado et Porturico with tenn peices of Brasse ordnance to entertaine us, hee alsoe prepared an Armado by Sea to sett uppon us, Itt weere to longe to tell you, how wee weere preserved, my braines are broken, and I cannot write much. I live yett, and I have told you why.

Whitney, for whome I sold my Plate att Plymouth, and to whome I gave more Creditt and Countenance, then to all the Captaynes of my Fleete, ranne from mee att the Granadoes, and Wolleston with him, Soe as I am nowe but five shipps, and one of those I have sent home, my ffly boate, and in her, a Rable of idle Rascalls ; which I knowe will not spare to wound mee, but I care not, I am sure there is never a base slave in the fleet hath taken the paines, and Care, that I have done, hath slept soe litle, and travailed soe much, My freinds will not beleive in them, and for the rest I Care not, God in heaven blesse you, and strengthen your heart.

Your W: Raleigh.

VI. [*A letter of Sir Walter Raleigh to the King from the Tower, September* 24, 1618.]

MAye it please your most excellent majestie.
    If in my Jorny outward bound I had of my men murthered at the Ilands and spared to take revenge, if I did discharge some Spanish barkes taken, without spoile, if I forbare all partes of the Spanish Indies wherin I might have taken twentie of their townes on the sea cost and did only follow the enterprise which I undertooke for Guiana, where without any direccion from me a Spanish village was burnt, which was newly sett up within three miles of the Mine.

By your majesties favor I finde noe reason whie the Spanish Embassadore should complaine of me. If it were lawfull for the Spanish to murther 26 Englishmen tyenge them back to backe and then to cutt theire throtes, when they had traded with them a whole moneth and came to them on the land without so much as one sword amongst them all, and if it may not be lawfull for your majesties subjects beinge forced by them, to repell force by force we may justly say Oh miserable English: If Parker and Mutton tooke Campeach and other places in the Honduraes seated in the hart of the Spanish Indies, burnt townes, killed the Spaniards, and had nothing sayed to them at their returne, and that my selfe forbore to looke into the Indies because I would not 10 offend. I may as justly say oh miserable Sir Walter Rawleigh. If I had spent my poore estate, lost my sonne, suffred by sicknes and otherwise a world of miseries, if I had resisted with the manifest hazard of my life the rebells and spoiles which my companyes would have made, if when I was poore I could have mad my selfe rich, if when I had gotten my libertye which all men and nature it selfe doth so much prise I voluntarilie lost it, if when I was master of my life I rendred it againe, if [when] I might elsewhere have sould my shipp and goods 20 and put five or six thousand pounds in my purse, I have brought her into England. I beseech your Majestie beleeve that all this I have done because it should be sayed to your Majestie that your majestie had given libertie and trust to a man whose ende was but the recovery of his libertie, and whoe had not betrayed your majesties trust.

My mutiners tould me that if I returned for England I should be undone, but I beleeved more in your majesties goodnes then in their arguments. Sure I am that I am 30 the first that being free and able to inrich my selfe, hath embraced povertie, and as sure I am that my example shall meke me the last. But your majesties wisdome and goodnes I have made my Judges whoe have ever bine and shall ever remain Your majesties

most humble Vassall

W. Rauleigh.

NOTE ON THE MAP

In 1596 Raleigh published *The Discoverie of the Large, Rich, and Bewtiful Empyre of Guiana, with a relation of the great and Golden Citie of Manoa (which the Spanyards call El Dorado) And of the Provinces of Emeria, Arromaia, Amapaia, and other Countries with their rivers, adjoyning. Performed in the yeare 1596. by Sir W. Ralegh Knight.* In the course of the work he referred to 'a large Chart or Map, which I have not yet finished'. This map is now preserved in the British Museum as Additional MS. 17940 A. A portion of it, showing the Orinoco, is here reproduced. It should be noted that the map is drawn upside down, with the North and the Atlantic Ocean at the bottom instead of the top. Raleigh entered by the Manamo mouth from the Bay of Guanipa, which he has marked ; and he rowed up into the Caroni. The coastline is accurately charted, but the river is rather vague. The mine, which was known to Kemish only, was near the junction of the Orinoco with the Caroni. A curious feature of the map is the vast inland sea, named the Lake of Manoa with the site of El Dorado, or the 'Golden City', approximately marked upon its shores. The lake is a geographical blunder due to the enormous floods in the low-lying ground of Venezuela during the rainy season. El Dorado was the object of many fruitless quests. Raleigh concluded his *Discovery* with a series of letters and reports attesting its existence ; he also states that 'on the lake of *Manoa*, and in a multitude of other rivers' gold is gathered 'in peeces as bigg as small stones' (p. 80), and that if Queen Elizabeth sent 'but a smal army' to march on Manoa, the native king 'would yeeld her Majesty by composition so many hundred thousand pounds yearely, as should both defende all enemies abroad, and defray all expences at home '.

NOTES

PAGE **25,** l. 30. *Baily* : Captain Baily afterwards achieved distinction as the proprietor of ' Baily's coaches ', the first hackney coaches to ply in London.

PAGE **36,** l. 25. *Siracides* : *Ecclesiasticus, The Wisdom of Jesus the Son of Sirach*, one of the books of the Apocrypha.

PAGE **37,** l. 20. *Mala opinio, &c.* : ' An ill-reputation is a delight if it be virtuously acquired.'

l. 25. *Sic vos non vobis* : ' So you produce for others, not for your selves.' An early life of Virgil says that a couplet written by him in honour of Augustus was stolen by a plagiarist, who secured a reward from the Emperor : Virgil then wrote out the verses with additional lines stating that he was the author, but had gained by them no more than a sheep gains from its wool or a bee from its honey.

> Sic vos non vobis vellera fertis, oves :
> Sic vos non vobis mellificatis, apes.

PAGE **40,** l. 18. *Hermes* : Hermes Trismegistus was the Greek name for Thoth, the Egyptian god of wisdom. A variety of mystical writings (sometimes called Hermetri) were attributed to him. One of these—a Latin treatise, ' On the Wisdom and Power of God '—was popular in the Middle Ages.

PAGE **42,** l. 7. *recovered* : in the obsolete sense of ' reached '. ' arrived at '.

PAGE **43,** l. 1. *eo crevit, &c.* : ' It has grown so much that it is burdened with its own greatness.'

l. 3. *Cratippus* : a peripatetic philosopher at Athens, who taught Cicero's son.

PAGE **45,** l. 2. *non obstante* : The first two words of a clause formerly used in letters patent, which conveyed a licence from the sovereign to do anything notwithstanding any statute to the contrary.

l. 25. *Beatitudo, &c.* : ' Happiness is not the knowledge of divine things, but the divine life.'

PAGE **46,** l. 17. *Materia prima* : primal matter, i. e. matter without form or qualities, the substance out of which, according to certain philosophers, the universe was made.

PAGE **47,** l. 11. *Master* Dannet : Thomas Danett, who translated Philip de Comines *Memoirs of Louis XI* (published in 1600), and issued in the same year *A Continuation of the Historie of France,* from which Raleigh quotes the anecdote of Seldius (p. 131 in the original). In l. 28 Raleigh abbreviates with an '&c.'; Danett continues, 'and that hee whom thou hast served so manye yeares hath also served thee and borne the candle downe before thee'.

PAGE **48,** l. 26. *Lactantius* : A Roman writer of the fourth century, sometimes called the Christian Cicero.

l. 27. *quod sapientes, &c.* : 'Because they are wise in a foolish matter.'

PAGE **50,** l. 1. *Divitias nulla, &c.* : 'Riches acquired without guile.'

PAGE **51,** l. 22. *O quam multi, &c.* : 'Oh ! how many with this hope enter the arena of eternal labours and wars.'

PAGE **52,** l. 17. *Cappe* : 'His cap . . . in which all men of any quality displayed either a brooch of gold or silver, was ornamented with a paltry image of the Virgin, in lead, such as the poorer sort of pilgrims bring from Loretto.' *Quentin Durward*, chap. ii.

PAGE **55,** l. 5. *Omnia quæ eventura, &c.* : 'All things in the future are uncertain.'

PAGE **56,** l. 2. *wise man* : Seneca, *De Remediis Fortuitorum*, xvi. 10.

l. 7. *qui gementes, &c.* : 'Who follow their general with lamentations.'

l. 18. *Footstoole of Tamerlane* : see Marlowe's *Tamburlaine the Great*, Pt. I, Act IV, Sc. ii :

> *Tamb.* Bring out my footstool.
>
> [*Bajazet is taken out of the cage.*
> *Tamb.* . . . Fall prostrate on the low disdainful earth
> And be the footstool of great Tamburlaine
> That I may rise into my royal throne.
>
> [*Tamburlaine gets up on him to his chair.*]

Bajazet I, Sultan of the Turks in the fourteenth century, was a famous conqueror, who overran Bulgaria and parts of Serbia, Macedonia, Thessaly, and the greater part of Asia Minor. He was defeated and taken prisoner by Timur, who in reality treated him with great generosity. Marlowe's play is based on a popular fiction which has no foundation in fact. The great national day of the Serbians—Kosovo Day (June 28)—was kept in memory of their defeat by Bajazet on the field of Kosovo Polje (1389) and of the regaining of their independence 500 years later.

l. 19. *Sapores* : Sapor I, son of Artaxerxes, king of Persia, defeated the Emperor Valerian and kept him a prisoner for life.

l. 20. *Bellisarius* : The most famous general of Justinian. He was of humble birth, but became one of the most noted men of his time. Justinian grew jealous of his fame, accused him of conspiracy, and, according to a popular legend, put out his eyes and reduced him to beggary. In reality he seems merely to have been imprisoned for a time in his own palace, and then restored to honour.

l. 23. *of the least*: so the text of 1614; 'as the least', later editions.

l. 30. *Magni ingenii, &c.* : 'It is the mark of a great character to withdraw the mind from the senses.'

PAGE **57,** l. 24. *directed*: probably by Prince Henry. See p. 62, l. 12.

PAGE **58,** l. 17. *Olympiads*: the Greek measure of time. The name comes from the Olympic Games, the four years from one festival to the next being called an Olympiad.

PAGE **60,** l. 20. *gracili avena* : 'With oaten (or slender) pipe.'

l. 25. *Montanus* : Arias Montanus, a famous Biblical scholar of the sixteenth century. He was proficient in Hebrew, Chaldean, Syriac, Arabic, Greek, and Latin, and spoke fluently French, German, Flemish, and Portuguese.

PAGE **62,** l. 5. *Unus mihi, &c.* : 'One man was to me as good as a whole people.' There is a Greek saying : 'One man is to me as ten thousand.'

l. 6. *Hoc ego, &c.* : 'This I intend, not for the multitude, but for you.'

l. 8. *Satis est unus, &c.* : 'If one's enough, none's enough.'

ll. 15–17. *Eadem probamus, &c.* : 'We are unanimous in approval, unanimous in blame : this is the upshot of every trial in which the dispute is submitted to more than one.'

PAGE **64,** l. 16. *concoct* : in its original sense of 'digest' (Lat. *concoquere*).

PAGE **65,** l. 11. *to that holy place* : so 1614; 'to seize that holy place', later editions.

PAGE **66,** l. 2. *women armed with tilestones*. Compare Judges ix. 53, 54 : 'And a certain woman cast a piece of a millstone upon Abimelech's head, and all to brake his skull. Then he called hastily unto the young man his armour-bearer and said unto him, "Draw thy sword and slay me, that men say not of me, 'A woman slew him'"'.'

l. 10. *opened the gates unto the French King* : Charles VIII entered Florence in 1494 : 'Wherever he went his heedless ignorance and the gross misconduct of his followers left behind implacable hostility' (*Encyclopaedia Brit.*).

PAGE **67,** l. 27. *distinction* : so in 1614 text ; 'intrusion' in later editions.

PAGE 72, l. 9. *Amurath*: Amurath II, emperor of the Turks, after a long career of conquest was defeated by the Christians in 1442. His son died immediately after the conclusion of peace, and Amurath was so overcome with grief that he abdicated. The Christians promptly renewed their attacks, and Amurath returned to power and defeated them, with great slaughter, at Varna, 1444.

PAGE 73, l. 6. *The winning of this passage*: Raleigh has just been describing how Alexander forced the passage of the Granicus.

PAGE 79, l. 26. *Rabanus*: Hrabanus Maurus Magnentius (776–856), sometimes called Rabanus, a well-known theological writer.

PAGE 80, ll. 4–7. *For whereas . . . make warre*: compare Sir John Mandeville's account of the Island of Taprobane: 'In this isle . . . be great hills of gold that pismires (ants) keep full diligently. . . . And these pismires be great as hounds, so that no man dare come to those hills, for the pismires would assail them and devour them anon. So that no man may get of that gold but by great sleight. And therefore when it is great heat, the pismires rest them in the earth from prime of the day into noon. And then the folk of the country take camels, dromedaries, and horses and other beasts, and go thither and charge them in all haste that they may ; and after that they flee away in all haste that the beasts may go, or the pismires come out of the earth.' (*Travels*, chap. xxxiii. 1356.)

PAGE 87, l. 1. *practised by Xerxes*: recorded by Raleigh in Book III. chap. vi. § 11 of the *Historie*. Xerxes, loving the wife of Masistes, who rejected him, handed her over to the vengeance of his own wife, who mutilated her ; Masistes, starting for Bactria, where he hoped to raise a rebellion, was intercepted and killed.

PAGE 92, l. 12. *Genowayes*: Genoese.

PAGE 94, l. 11. *Syphax*: king of Numidia in the Second Punic War.

l. 13. *Perseus*: the last king of Macedonia, conquered by Aemilius, Paulus at Pydna, 168 B.C.

l. 14. *Gentius*: king of Illyria, and an ally of Perseus. He was defeated in battle and surrendered to Anicius, who carried him to Rome to adorn his triumph.

PAGE 95, l. 16. *braverie*: i. e. bravado, swaggering.

l. 22. *two hundred*: so 1614 ; 'five hundred' later editions.

PAGE 98, l. 11. *maritimate*: Raleigh frequently uses this word for 'maritime'.

l. 18. *bankes*: i. e. the bench on which the rowers sit in a galley.

PAGE 100, l. 13. *accidentally*: added in later editions.

l. 23. *during*: i. e. power of endurance.

l. 30. *Peter Strossie*: cf. p. 110, l. 19.   Peter Strozzi was a member of the famous Florentine house which greatly distinguished itself in arms in the sixteenth century.

PAGE **102**, l. 13. *Hermocrates*: one of the chief citizens of Syracuse at the time of the Athenian invasion (fifth century B. C.). When the Syracusians had been defeated by land, Hermocrates urged them to try their fortune again by sea.

l. 24. *Curæ leves, &c.* : ' Light griefs find utterance ; deep griefs are dumb' (Seneca).

PAGE **103**, l. 24. *Count Maurice of Nassau* : eldest son of William of Orange, and one of the most famous generals of the day : ' If the United Provinces owed their prosperity to Holland, they owed their very existence to the House of Orange. Had it not been for the statesmanship of William the Silent they would never have won their independence, had it not been for the generalship of Maurice they would never have maintained it.' (Wakeman, *European History*, Period V, p. 219.)

PAGE **104**, l. 28. *Sir John Norris* : one of the bravest and most distinguished Elizabethan soldiers. He fought under Coligny in France, in Ireland, and in the Low Countries. In 1589 he and Drake were put in command of the expedition sent to destroy the shipping on the coasts of Spain and Portugal and to place the pretender, Don Antonio, on the Portuguese throne. Norris landed troops at Corunna, and afterwards directed an attack on Lisbon, but the enemy succeeded in avoiding a general engagement, and the expedition returned to Plymouth without having achieved anything decisive.

l. 30. *Lysborne* : Lisbon.

PAGE **105**, l. 9. *Groine* : Corunna.

PAGE **106**, l. 14. *a learned Gentleman* : Clement Edmondes, *Observations upon Cæsar's Commentaries* (1600 and 1604). The tactical problem here discussed is characteristic of the *Observations* and anticipates similar discussions by Raleigh himself in his *Historie*.

PAGE **107**, l. 4. *Marshall Monluc* : Blaise de Monluc, or Montluc, was a well-known soldier and the author of seven volumes of *Commentaires*, or Memoirs of his military career. His work is full of suggestions and advice for officers, and Henry IV called it ' la Bible des soldats '.

l. 13. *Monsieur de Langey* : Guillaume du Bellay, Sieur de Langey, famous soldier of the sixteenth century, and the author of several well-known works including Memoirs of his own time.

PAGE **110,** l. 29. *prevented* : forestalled. Cf. the collect beginning, ' Prevent us, O Lord, in all our doings.'

PAGE **112,** l. 25. *rest* : the old heavy muskets were fixed on rests stuck in the ground, in order to ensure steadiness of aim.

PAGE **114,** l. 25. *the greatest* : so in 1614 text ; ' these great ' in later editions.

PAGE **115,** l. 3. *Cineas* (fourth century B. c.), said to be the most eloquent speaker of his day, was the friend and minister of the famous conqueror Pyrrhus, king of Epirus.

PAGE **117,** l. 3. *to restore Navarre* : to the French.

l. 5. *Murderers of the Protestants* : Francis I (1494–1547) first persecuted the Protestants in his kingdom, but afterwards issued an edict of toleration. At the end of his life he once more attacked the Protestants, and in 1545 an edict was promulgated expelling the Waldenses from Provence.

PAGE **118,** l. 3. *Versa est, &c.* : Job xxx. 31 : ' My harp also is turned to mourning, and my organ into the voice of them that weep.'

l. 6. *Battle of Salamis* : 480 B. c. According to Herodotus, the Greek fleet numbered 378 ; most Greek writers say 300 or 310, of which the Athenians contributed 180. The Persian fleet appears to have numbered about 700, though most classical writers place the number as high as 1,200. At all events the numerical superiority was tremendous. Themistocles, the Athenian commander, was mainly instrumental in defeating the Persians, though the Greek fleet as a whole was under the command of Eurybiades, the Spartan.

PAGE **124,** l. 24. *all night* : so 1614 text ; ' all that night ', later editions.

PAGE **127,** l. 22. *Epaminondas* : a famous Theban general and statesman. The battle described in the text occurred in his fourth campaign in the Peloponnesus (362 B. c.). He raised Thebes to the supremacy of Greece, which she lost again soon after his death.

PAGE **133,** l. 18. *How the Illyrians infested the coast of Greece* : 231 B. c.

PAGE **135,** l. 21. *Agrigentum* : a town on the south coast of Sicily.

l. 22. *Eryx* : a mountain in Sicily, crowned by a famous temple of Aphrodite.

PAGE **136,** l. 18. *Nations* : so 1614 text ; ' sorts ' in later editions.

PAGE **137,** l. 15. *unmannerly* : so 1614 text ; omitted in some later editions.

PAGE **139**, l. 9. *was secure of the Romans*: i. e. felt secure with regard to them.

PAGE **144**, l. 2. *last summer*: 'the last of August 1591', Hakluyt.

PAGE **145**, l. 7. *240*: Hakluyt corrects to 140 (see p. 30).
l. 9. *Argosies*: large ships, said to take their name from Ragusa (Aragouse).
Caractes: ('Caracks', Hakluyt), large ships used by the Portuguese both for war and for trading with the East Indies.
Florentines: Florentine ships.
l. 12. *most*: omitted by Hakluyt.
conduction: 'conduct', Hakluyt.
l. 29. *they*: added by Hakluyt.

PAGE **146**, l. 9. *Pinnes*: pinnace, a small two-masted vessel.
l. 21. *made*: 'they made', Hakluyt.
l. 26. *or ostentation*: 'of ostentation', Hakluyt.

PAGE **147**, l. 10. *first*: omitted by Hakluyt.
l. 13. *three Pinnasses*: 'three other Pinnasses', Hakluyt.
l. 26. *pestered*: busied with numerous occupations.
l. 27. *romaging*: see note to p. 156, l. 16.

PAGE **148**, l. 20. *waied*: 'that wayed', Hakluyt.

PAGE **149**, l. 4. *luffe*: i. e. put down the helm so that the ship went head to wind.
l. 14. *carged*: high-carved, i. e. standing high out of the water.
l. 15. *after laid the* Revenge *aboord*: to lay a ship aboard is to place one's own ship alongside.
l. 19. *Brittan Dona*: here, and at p. 155, l. 16, Hakluyt spells 'Brittandona'.
l. 22. *chase*: the chase-ports, where the chase-guns were placed, were at the bow and stern of the ship, i. e. at the extreme ends.

PAGE **150**, l. 15. *Armados*: here, and in all later passages, Hakluyt spells 'Armadas'.

PAGE **152**, ll. 22–4. *The* Revenge . . . *sea*: Hakluyt simplifies the punctuation by printing these parenthetical words in brackets.
l. 30. *fifteene thousand*: Hakluyt corrects, 'above ten thousand'.

PAGE **153**, l. 16. *that where*: 'whereas', Hakluyt.
l. 28. *Bassen*: here, and elsewhere, Hakluyt spells 'Baçan'.

PAGE **155**, l. 2. *bewailed*: 'bewailing', Hakluyt.
l. 18. *Cutino*: 'Coutinho', Hakluyt.
l. 19. *two thousand*: Hakluyt corrects, 'one thousand'.

PAGE **156**, l. 15. *foul* applies to the outside of the ship, which was probably overgrown with weed and barnacles : *unroomaged* to the inside. The Custom House men still speak of rummaging when they overhaul a ship's cargo.

PAGE **157**, l. 21. *Michaels* : 'Michael', Hakluyt, here and on p. 165, l. 28.

    l. 22. *renowned* : 'renowmed', Hakluyt.

PAGE **159**, l. 30. *manners* : 'Mannors', Hakluyt.

PAGE **160**, ll. 3, 4. Hakluyt punctuates, 'others (all ... yeeres) was '.

PAGE **161**, l. 30. *naturall* : native.

PAGE **162**, l. 7. *The Spanish cruelties* : a tract by de las Casas, 'the Apostle of the Indies'—*Brevissima relacion de la destruycion de las Indias*—was published at Seville in 1552. Raleigh's title evidently refers to the French version of this, published at Antwerp in 1579—*Tyrannie et cruautez des Espagnols, perpetrees ès Indes Occidentales . . . fidelement traduictes par Iaques de Miggrode*. This French version was in its turn rendered into English in *The Spanishe Colonie, or Briefe Chronicle of the Acts & gestes of the Spaniards in the West Indies . . . written in the Castilian tongue by B. de las Casar . . . And nowe first translated into english by M. M. S.* (London, 1583). A Dutch version was published at Amsterdam in 1596, and at Frankfort there was a German version in 1597 and a Latin version in 1598.

    l. 28. *or religion* : 'and religion', Hakluyt.

PAGE **165**, ll. 7 sqq. Hakluyt smoothes out this ungrammatical sentence by reading at the beginning, 'The whole 77. ships joyned '. The change is interesting as showing how carefully he read his texts. For ' togither ' (l. 9) he reads ' all together '.

PAGE **167**, l. 2. *A Relation of Cadiz Action* : it is interesting to note that this vivid report was written by Raleigh immediately after the action : note the expression (p. 177, l. 5), ' we *purpose* to bring into England '. No doubt Raleigh wrote on board when he was ' unfit for aught but ease ' (p. 176, l. 11).

    l. 10. *My Lord Admiral* : Lord Howard of Effingham.

PAGE **168**, l. 24. *Entramos* : Spanish for ' We are going in '.

PAGE **170**, l. 19. *Curtain* : the wall of a fortified place, connecting two towers.

    l. 20. *Culverin* : large cannon.

PAGE **171,** l. 25. *Blurr* : blare.

PAGE **172,** l. 10. *fly-boats* : originally the name given to small boats used on the Vlie, or channel leading out of the Zuyder Zee. In English Vlie became confused with ' fly ' : hence a light, fast boat.

PAGE **174,** ll. 3, 4. *layd out a warp* : laid a thick rope ready to throw to the *Philip* to make her fast to Raleigh's own ship.

PAGE **177,** l. 20. *hyrte himselfe in the tower* : Raleigh tried to kill himself with a table-knife the day after his arrival in the Tower, but he only succeeded in inflicting a slight wound. On the authenticity of the letter, see p. 31. The text has been slightly corrected in a few points of punctuation, more especially in substituting a full-stop for a comma at the end of a sentence.

PAGE **179,** l. 5. *Lord Harry* : Lord Henry Howard.

l. 25. *Feoffees* : a legal term for a person to whom a freehold estate is conveyed in trust for someone else.

PAGE **182,** 11–13. *my honest Cosen . . . therein* : the Harley MS. reads ' as divers can witnesse ' : so the copy in the State Papers, but with the absurd reading ' dust ' for ' divers '.

ll. 14–15. *have thus Cruelly murthered mee* : less strong in the other MSS. : ' who desired my slaughter ', Harleian ; ' that desire my slaughter ', State Papers.

ll. 17–20 are omitted in the copy in the State Papers ; and Harleian MS. omits ' And I plainely perceive . . . day '.

l. 23. *my office of wynes* : in 1584 Raleigh had been granted ' the Farm of Wines ', i.e. the power to grant licences for the sale of wines and, subject to certain restrictions, to control their price. He sublet this right for a time to one, Richard Brown, who paid him £700 a year for the privilege. The largest amount Raleigh himself received in one year from this ' farm ' was £1,200.

PAGE **183,** l. 11. 200^{li} : ' a 7000^{li} ', Harleian MS.

ll. 12–13. *Besides . . . debts* : omitted in Harleian MS.

ll. 29–30. *Gett . . . wherein* and page **184,** ll. 1, 2, *Butt itt . . . begging itt* : omitted in State Papers and Harleian transcripts.

PAGE **184,** l. 5. *shapes* : ' formes ', State Papers and Harleian MS.

l. 11. *if the Land Continue* : omitted in State Papers and Harleian MS.

ll. 14–15. *The everlasting . . . Almightie God* : ' The everlasting, infinite, powerfull and inscrutable God ', State Papers ; ' The everlasting God powerfull infinite and unscrutable God almighty ', Harleian MS.

ll. 22–5. omitted in the State Papers ; ll. 22–3 omitted in the Harleian MS.

PAGE **185,** *IV* : Sir Ralph Winwood was dead when this letter reached England ; his death was a serious misfortune to Raleigh, to whom he was friendly. Other transcripts of the letter are found in the Harleian and Sloane MSS. (see p. 32) : the principal variants of those MSS. are quoted below :

l. 7. *and sharpest* : omitted in H. and S.

l. 12. *violent* : omitted in H. and S.

l. 14. *Bravo*, or Brava : the southernmost of the Cape Verde islands. H. and S. misread ' Prano '.

l. 16. *hurlican* : hurricane. ' Hurlicano ' in H.

l. 23. *shallups* : small open boats for river navigation.

l. 25. *assisted* : ' cherished ', H. and S.

l. 28. *without hope* : omitted in H. and S., which read ' these 6 weeks '.

PAGE **186,** l. 1. *then* : than. Cf. l. 24.

l. 10. *Chudlay* : H. and S. spell ' Chidley '. Cf. p. **187,** l. 19.

l. 16. *singular* : ' infinite ', H. and S.

l. 25. *all respect . . . hath* : ' all the respects of this world have ', H. and S.

PAGE **187,** l. 2. *Hamden* : ' Heydon ', S.

l. 5. *Way* : ' Wraye ', H. ; ' Wrey ', S.

l. 6. *Mr. William Herbert* : omitted in H. and S.

l. 14. *I must confesse, that* : om. H. ; ' I dare say that ' ,S.

l. 20. *the Armada* : ' their Armado ', H. and S. So l. 26.

l. 24. *defence at all for a* : ' force at all for the ', H. and S.

l. 25. *and to have dyed there* : omitted in H. and S.

PAGE **188,** l. 7. *Madril* : H. spells ' Madrid ', and so does S. at l. 9, keeping ' Madril ' here. Both forms were in contemporary use.

l. 12. *the 17th of May* : H. and S. date ' the second of May '.

l. 13. *a Caravell to* : ' a Coronell of ', H. and S. Coronell = colonel.

l. 18. *brought* : ' sent ', H. and S.

l. 25. *traded* : ' traded to ', H. and S. Cf. Hakluyt, *Voyages*, 1598, vol. i, p. 458, ' At the humble sute of the English merchants trading those countreys '.

l. 28. *torment* : ' Cruel torment ', H. and S.

PAGE **189,** ll. 3, 4. *I know . . . having lost* : S. has an important variant : ' I knowe his Majestie (whom I am to satisfye) expects not at my hands soe much, my selfe haveing lost.' H. at this point is ungrammatical.

l. 6. *passages* : ' passage ', H. and S.

l. 9. *aspera et fragosa* : rough and broken. S., for the second adjective, has ' nemorosa ' (= wooded), and H. makes an attempt at the same word with ' Nemosa '.

    l. 10. *rivers* : ' river ', H. and S.
    l. 13. *Bankes* : ' boate ', H. and S.
    l. 15. *in the heade* : om. H. and S.
    l. 20. *hardly able* : ' not able ', H. and S.
    l. 21. *alarmes and* : om. H. and S.
    l. 22. *that* : ' that the mine ', H. and S.
    l. 30. *neither can they* : ' nor can ', H. and S.

PAGE **190,** l. 4. *Quinto* : a fifth part of any finds or any acquired treasure paid as a due to the King of Spain.

    l. 15. *lost*: ' slaine ', H. and S., which also read, ' if I had lost ' for ' if he had lost '.

    l. 27. *whether any other Prince or State* : the French ambassador had made overtures to Raleigh before he left England (see Introduction, p. 24) ; H. and S. have here a significant variant : ' whether my Prince will give '. Most of the readings in these MSS. suggest that they are copied from an earlier draft ; but the change in this passage suggests editing.

PAGE **191,** l. 4. *weake bodie* : ' sicke body ', H. and S.
    ll. 12–13. *when they were . . . thence* : om. H. and S.
    l. 19. *my patent* : ' my harte ', H., probably misreading the word ; ' my harts desire ', S., probably trying to make sense of this reading.

    l. 20. *was non ens* : ' had no existence '.
    l. 21. *he* : ' they ', H. and S.
    l. 22. *when* : ' but when ', H. and S.
    l. 25. *that* : ' but ', H. and S.
    l. 29. *with litle losse* : here H. omits ' little ', and S. emends ' without losse '.

PAGE **192,** l. 9. *the bullet* : om. H. and S.
    l. 12. *in a fly-boate* : om. H. and S.
    l. 14. *other* : om. H. and S.
    l. 17. *scumme* : ' scorne ', H. and S.
    l. 18. *paine* : ' paines ', H. and S. Cf. p. 197, l. 5.
    l. 20. *if I live* : om. H. and S.

PAGE **193,** l. 13. *Deare* : ' Deerest ', Harleian MS.
    ll. 24–5. *Comend . . . Loathbury* : om. H.

PAGE **194,** l. 13. *with sorrowe* : after these words the Harleian MS. has, ' for your sake in hope to provide somewhat for you ; and to comfort ', &c.

    l. 25. *a Company* : in H., ' a Company of Rascalls '.

PAGE **196**, ll. 2–3. H. omits 'But because . . . then any other', running on, ' I referr you to knowe the truth'.

l. 7. *and to Sir John Leigh* : om. H.

l. 25. *preserved* : H. adds, ' if I live I shall make it knowne'.

PAGE **198**, l. 4. *forced* : ' chardged first ', Harleian MS.

ll. 6–7. *other places in the Honduraes* : om. H.

l. 15. *rebells* : ' robberies ', H.

ll. 16–17. *if when I was poore . . . rich* : om. H.

l. 19. *master* : ' Sure ', H.

l. 26. *not betrayed* : ' betrayed ', H., a tempting correction of the text.

PAGE **199**, l. 2. *povertie* : H. adds, ' and perill '.

Printed in England at the Oxford University Press